Secure Me

How to Live Securely in an Insecure World

Kevin Scruggs

ISBN 978-1-63874-592-1 (paperback)
ISBN 978-1-63874-593-8 (digital)

Christian Faith Publishing, Inc.
832 Park Avenue
Meadville, PA 16335
www.christianfaithpublishing.com

Printed in the United States of America

To my wife, Monica, since the moment I saw you across the room in the summer of 1991, I knew you were the one for me. Thank you for all the wisdom and love you have shown me over almost thirty years of being together. I'm a better man because of it. Every day with you is a gift from God. I love you. Cross my heart.

To my girls, I have loved being your dad since the moment you were born. You truly are a blessing in my life. I can't wait to see the wonderful plans God has for your life.

To Jeff, thank you for being a catalyst in my life to get this book written. Time on the couch in your office and the tools you've given me have helped in ways I can't even begin to express.

To Anni, thanks for being my ghost reader and for pushing me to finish this book. I'm grateful for your friendship.

Contents

Foreword

Hi, I'm Jeff. You will hear about me in a few chapters. Kevin has written from his heart and opened himself up to us in vulnerable ways through this book. His journey mirrors that of our own. He has invited us to face our own insecurities by looking within and challenging us to seek a God who offers an answer to our very personal questions and struggles about our insecurities and how to live securely in Him.

As a therapist, I think a person's insecurities are often a theme in therapy. We all have them. It's what you do with them that makes the difference. This is a book that will not only help you grow in your own personal journey but would also be an excellent resource for someone you care about that struggles with their own insecurities.

I hope, over these next pages, you will take steps forward on your path of living a "secure me" life, every single day.

—Dr. Jeff McFarlane
Psychologist, PsyD
Clinical Director of Restoration Counseling Services

Introduction

I wrote parts of this introduction over two years ago. This is a book that has been over ten years in the making. I can't tell you how many times I have tried to start this book. Each year, when my birthday odometer flips over, the same goal is staring me in the face—to write this book. This year, I turned fifty. Talk about insecurity. Recently, I've watched our world turn upside down from this global pandemic. It's interesting to see where people have placed their security and how they have reacted when it fell apart. Security versus Insecurity. The story of our lives.

Every bad decision I have ever made in my life has come from insecurity—from relationships, finances, places I've gone to, things I have purchased, even my own stuff with God. The crazy part is that we react out of insecurity to try and feel secure, which only leads to more insecurity. It is a life that you and I were never meant to live. I believe that everyone struggles with insecurity at some level, we just live it out in different ways. It's a story as old as time. Back in the beginning, before the fig leaves, the Bible says that man and woman walked with God. They hung out with Him. Then one day, they were told by a serpent that God was holding out on them. It didn't matter what they had already experienced with God. This new "revelation" hit a nerve buried deep inside. *Hello, insecurity!* You and I have been living with that decision ever since. I'm on this journey of realizing that I don't have to live that way. You don't have to live that way. God has something more.

I can already hear you, "This is one of those religious books. Moving on." Before you go, let me ask you something. What if you could live a secure life, would you be interested? What if you could make decisions out of security and still be comfortable in your own skin? I believe that is possible.

Don't worry, this isn't a self-help book nor are you about to join a cult. This is a story about my journey and, more than likely, your journey too. It's a story that has been repeated millions of times over. I would like to invite you to come along for the ride. I think you might be surprised how it turns out. Who knows, you may find some of your own story along the way. Maybe lots of people will read it this book, or maybe just my mom. Either way, I've got to get this off my to-do list while my eyes and my hearing are still mostly good. So here we go.

Secure Me… living the life we were always meant to live.

1

Securely Insecure

I have wanted to start this book at least a hundred times. I have known that this was something I was supposed to write about and share with you, but the thought of talking about insecurity with other people is the very definition of insecurity. Every human being struggles with insecurity, every single person who has ever taken a breath, but we don't want to admit it. Honestly one of the biggest roadblocks in writing this stuff is being labeled as that insecure guy who wrote that book. You may be reading this book in secret because you don't want anyone to know about your insecurities either.

I've realized something on my journey. You are just as insecure about your life as I am about mine. How we live out those insecurities may look different, true, but at the core of it all, we are all the same. Let me say it a different way. Every bad decision I have ever made in my life has come out of insecurity. My guess is, you have a similar story. Insecurity lived out is compromises we make to feel better. We go places we shouldn't go, try things we shouldn't try, make purchases we can't afford, and say things shouldn't say usually to fit in with a group of people we may not even like. We cross lines in relationships to feel loved and accepted. We may buy something we can't afford to feel like we are somebody. We post pictures on our social media at just the right angle and in the best light. We spend a ridiculous amount of time positioning ourselves in such a way to feel secure about our place in the world, and it's exhausting.

Insecurity shows up in every corner of our lives. Relationships, finances, work, marriage, family, places we go, things we purchase, our social media accounts, even in our responses to hurt, anger, or sadness. How am I doing so far? The pattern usually goes something like this—I'm feeling insecure about something, so I make a decision out of that insecurity to gain some type of control and feel secure. That control is temporary, which then leads to regret and eventually, even more insecurity. It's a never-ending cycle. It's a cycle we were never meant to experience. With all that as our backdrop, let me start at the beginning.

Hi, my name is Kevin, and I struggle with insecurity. Now that we have that out of the way, let's walk down this path together. Have you ever looked up the definition of security and insecurity?

- *secure* \si-'kyur\ (adjective)
  1. a. easy in mind: *confident*
     b. assured in opinion or expectation: having no doubt
  2. a. free from danger
     b. free from risk of loss

- *insecure* \ˌin-si-'kyur\ (adjective)
  Etymology, from medieval Latin *insecurus*, *in* + *securus* (secure)
  1. not confident or sure: *uncertain* (feeling somewhat *insecure* of his reception)
  2. not adequately guarded or sustained: *unsafe* (an *insecure* investment)
  3. not firmly fastened or fixed: *shaky* (the hinge is loose and *insecure*)
  4. a. not highly stable or well-adjusted (an *insecure* marriage)

b. deficient in assurance: beset by fear and anxiety
    (always felt *insecure* in a group of strangers)

Merriam-Webster's Collegiate Dictionary, 11th ed. (Springfield, MA: 2003), Merriam-Webster, Inc.

The first one is the goal. The second one is more reality. Let me break it down into a usable definition. *Security* is to be "relived from exposure to danger." *Insecurity* is to "not be adequately guarded; not confident."—the relief from danger versus the risk of exposure to danger.

Let me ask you something. Where is your security right now? What makes you feel secure? Maybe it's a roof over your head, food in your fridge, a relationship, a job, money in the bank, or your health. These are not necessarily bad things. It's the American dream, right? What would happen if some or all of those things were taken away? How would you react? What would you do to get it back? At the end of the day, we just want to feel better. These are the things that help us accomplish that goal. When our life gets out of balance, we take steps to bring things back into order. Control equals security. Most of the time, we do it without even thinking about it. Think about the last time one of your security pieces was out of balance. Fear starts creeping in. Life is a little unstable. We lose sleep. We feel stress. Time for action! So we do, say, or move toward our solution to bring security back into our lives. It's a cycle that looks something like this:

Option 1:
feeling insecure—want security
    the *pursuit* - my insecurity (I'm feeling inse-
      cure and I want to feel secure)
    the *pivot* - my control (I will make decisions
      to control something to feel secure)
    the *payoff* - more insecurity (temporary satis-
      faction > more difficulties)

My control leads to my (bad) decision, which leads to my (temporary) security, which leads to even more difficulties, which leads to insecurity…(and the cycle repeats). When you start with a faulty premise, you can eventually expect faulty results.

The bottom line is that I just want to feel better and who knows better than me on how to accomplish that goal? The problem is that our *feeling* of security is temporary because we made a bad decision, hoping for a good result that we think we can control. Eventually, that falls apart and makes the situation worse, which often leads to more insecurity and makes us feel even worse than when we started. Let's just say that I have firsthand knowledge of this crazy ride. Remember what I said earlier, every bad decision that I have ever made in my life has come out of insecurity with a desire to control my sense of security. Let's use an easy example. You are feeling lonely so you go somewhere to meet people. You are feeling good and find yourself zeroing in on one person in particular with whom you feel a connection (pursuit). As the night progresses, the bond is stronger. Let's throw in some liquid courage to help this along. You decide to spend the night together (pivot). Now in the moment, you don't feel lonely at all. In the moment you feel pretty amazing. The next day, you replay the previous night and fear or regret creeps in (payoff). You ask yourself some questions, "Who was this person? Will they call? Did they give me something I don't want? What was I thinking?" Suddenly, the euphoria of security is gone and is replaced by an even greater insecurity than if you had just stayed home and watched Netflix. You can run the same cycle in financial deals, relationships, social media responses, honestly pretty much in every area of our lives. There, now don't you feel better? Yeah, me neither. What if I told you that there was another option. What if we could stop repeating this cycle over and over, hoping that one day it gets better? Would you be interested?

Read on, my friend. This is where I'm going to ask you to trust me because what you are about to read may sound more fantasy than reality. This may be the point where some of you will roll your eyes, put the book the book down, and send me a nice e-mail. I get it. Here is the truth. I've been on both sides of this equation. I've helped people who are on both sides of this equation. All I can tell you is that option 2 is the better option. I've see it in others and I've experienced it myself. I'll explain it in more detail in the next chapter, but it looks something like this.

> Option 2:
> feeling insecure - want security
>> the *pursuit* - we surrender control
>> the *pivot* - which leads to peace
>> the *payoff* - which yields more security

Let's go back through our scenario. You are feeling lonely so you go somewhere to meet people. But this time, you ask yourself *where is a good place to go to meet people.* You are feeling good and find yourself zeroing in on one person in particular with whom you feel a connection. At this point, you begin to ask yourself a series of questions that come from somewhere inside of you (surrender control). *Is this where I find my satisfaction? My security? What are the long-term impacts of tonight? Will liquid courage help or hurt my decision-making process?* As the night progresses, the bond becomes stronger. You have already decided that no matter what, you are going home alone tonight because this is not where my security will be found tomorrow morning (leads to peace). My security cannot not come from a one-night stand. Maybe you exchange numbers, maybe you thank them for a fun evening. The next day, you replay the previous night and decide if you want to contact them or not. There are no ties and no expectations, just a fun evening. You wake up the next morning with no regrets and realize that you are okay (more security).

Yes, you still don't like feeling lonely. Yes, you are still alone, but you are secure in just being you. Someday the right relationship will come along with the right person in the right way. Both of these scenarios are realistic. It all happens in the pivot. We decide where and what will provide us security. One causes us to focus on the short-term satisfaction that depends solely on our control, while the other causes us to surrender our control and causes us to continue to lean back into *Something* that is greater than ourselves. At the end of the day, we get to decide the ending.

I know this doesn't make sense right now, and I'm certainly not trying to sound all mystical. That's why I'm asking you to trust me and keep reading. I'm not writing this book as someone who has "arrived." I write this book as a beggar showing other beggars where to find bread. I'm sitting here as a fifty-year-old man who has made plenty of mistakes but has also experienced some really cool victories as well. It has all hinged on the pivot, option 1 or option 2. It really is that simple…but also that hard. For you and me to experience security, real security, we will have to decide if we want to try and be in control (and we know how that ends) or surrender control to *Someone* else. Yes that "s" is capitalized on purpose.

I'm not going to sit here and blow sunshine and tell you that if you choose option 2, *everything* is going to be okay. That's a lie. The reality is that we are going to face difficulties no matter what. Relationships end. People get sick. The stock market rises and falls. No one gets through life unscathed. That's reality. I wish my life could be more like my dog who is curled up next to me as I write this page. His biggest concerns are making sure he gets food, there is water in his dish, and having his belly scratched. Never underestimate the value of a good belly scratch. My dog's life is pretty good. Our lives are not always like that. We have seasons of good and seasons of difficulty. That's life. We can't change that. What we can change is where we place our security. It's that spot in our lives that never seems to be satisfied with all the things we try put in it. Fame, fortune, health, relationships, our career, even followers on social media are all temporary. Sounds crazy, but it's true.

Let me give you an example. I have two daughters. When they started school, I began a tradition of interviewing them about their first day of school. The same questions, the same interview, every year on their first day of school. When they graduated from high school, we put the clips together and put it out on the Internet. Yes, I'm that dad. My voice may be famous, but my girls got all the attention. Much to our surprise, the videos went viral with roughly 80 million views and counting across various social media platforms. One of them even trended at number 2 on YouTube. Both times, we had a very similar experience. When the videos dropped, we did all kinds of interviews for TV, magazines, and newspapers. My girls were recognized when they went out. We had people contacting us from all around the world. Talk shows mentioned our video. Even Ryan Seacrest mentioned it on his radio show. Not gonna lie, I geeked out on that one. It was all pretty cool…for about two weeks, until the next big thing came across the Internet. It was a weird feeling have all this attention and notoriety and then *poof!* It was gone. Nobody calls us for interviews anymore. My kids can walk out in public without being recognized. The YouTube clicks have dropped off to almost nothing. Honestly, I don't know how celebrities do it.

Here's the point. All the stuff we put into our lives to help us feel secure is temporary. All of it. It's the reason we keep going on the insecurity cycle that only leads to more insecurity. So how do I change it? It's all in the pivot, that moment we make a decision to head in one direction or another. Option 1 yields temporary satisfaction but in the end provides only greater insecurity. Option 2 sounds scary at first but ultimately provides us with peace. Choosing Option 2 will require giving up control, which makes no sense, unless you place it in the One who controls it all. It's the relationship you and I were always meant to have. Come walk with me for a minute. I'll show you what I mean.

2

~~~

The Best Day We Never Saw

I love good conversation. One of my favorite things to do is sit on my back porch with a glass of wine, with my favorite smooth jazz playing in the background, and just talk with my friends. I think everyone has a story to tell.

I want you to think back to one of the best moments of your life. Start right at the beginning. What are you wearing? Was there anything particularly special about that day? Where did this moment take place? Were you with someone or by yourself? What were some of the smells you remember? What was the best part of your perfect moment? Let's take a pause here. Feel the emotions. Allow the smile to come across your face. Perhaps it's been a while since you thought about it. Don't rush ahead. This will make sense in a minute. Do you have that moment in your head? Perfect. Now hold that thought.

My turn. One of the best meals I've ever had was the only time I've been to Hawaii. We were on vacation with some friends on the island of Kauai. It was one of the best vacations I've ever experienced. The week was perfect. Something you should know about me is that I'm a foodie. I'm an atmosphere-and-good-conversation kind of guy. A few days before we left to return home, we wanted to go to this very special restaurant right on the beach. We had to make reservations earlier in the week. The view was breathtaking! In fact, they give you sunglasses to wear at your table because it is so bright when the sun sets over the ocean. We were given the best table in the restaurant. I remember I had the mahi-mahi with a macadamia nut crust. I can still taste it. During the meal, we excused ourselves to go outside and take pictures of the sunset. The sky looked like a painting. It was like nothing I had ever seen. Speaking of beauty, my wife completely took my breath away. We have a picture of us kissing under a palm tree with this incredible sunset backdrop. There isn't one thing I would change about that evening. It was something that I will never forget.

My *moment* was probably a lot like yours. When you think of it, you smile. Picture it in your mind. It's a good memory. Now I want to ask you another question. How would your moment have changed if the person in your life who has hurt you the deepest, just happened to step into the picture? Would it still be one of the best moments or would it suddenly, without warning, become one of the worst. If that person had been my waiter or sat at the table next to me, would I have even shared it with you? Probably not. How is it that one person can change the best moment into the worst? Actually, it's part of our original story. Regardless of what you believe about the origin of man, I think we can all agree that mankind as a species does bad things that impacts others. For just a moment, I want to ask you to step on to the same page with me. Let's listen to someone else's perfect day and how it all went terribly wrong.

In the book of Genesis, we read the story of Adam and Eve. The Bible says that God created them and everything around them. It was…perfect. Man and woman lacked for nothing. Every day, every moment was absolutely perfect. Their relationship with each other was amazing. No fights, no disagreements. Every interaction was satisfying. They had plenty to eat. They had no stress. They didn't need to worry about anything. Every day was filled with security. This is how God created it to be. It was His original plan for mankind. Man and woman not only had a perfect relationship with each other, they also had a perfect relationship with God. The Bible says that they walked with God. They hung out with Him. I bet they asked God all kinds of questions about what He made. I bet they laughed, played games, and really enjoyed each other's company. Maybe even listened to some smooth jazz. There was no fear, no sadness, no pretending or trying to impress anyone. They felt secure in every area of their lives. Perfectly secure. It's something that you and I can't imagine because every relationship we have every experienced has had a little bit of bad in it because there is a little bad in all of us. I'm getting ahead of myself.

One morning, something changed. There came another perfect day in Eden when Eve had a conversation with someone else. The Bible calls him a serpent. This serpent asked Eve a question about her relationship with God. You see, God told Adam and Eve that they could eat anything they wanted in this garden, except for the tree of the knowledge of good and evil. Up until this point, they had just leaned into their relationship with God and each other and said, "No problem." Basically, they just stayed away from that tree because their security rested in God. The serpent began to ask Eve some questions about God's request. Eve responded in kind. Then the serpent made a suggestion to Eve. "Eve, God is holding out on you. He doesn't want you to eat from it because if you do, you will be like God." For the first time in her life, Eve took her focus off of God and onto the tree. She moved her security from God (who made and provided everything she needed) and placed it on something she thought was better than God (something she thought she could control). She decided her security would be found in something better. It would be her decision. When she took that first bite, along with her husband, Adam, there was this brief moment that they thought they had it. Then suddenly, their perfect world of security came crashing down around them. That's the day mankind experienced sin, something God never wanted them to experience. At that moment, insecurity was front and center in their lives.

Genesis 3 describes it this way, "So when the woman saw that the tree was good for food, and that it was a delight to the eyes, and that the tree was to be desired to make one wise, she took of its fruit and ate, and she also gave some to her husband who was with her, and he ate. Then the eyes of both were opened, *and they knew that they were naked*. And they sewed fig leaves together and made themselves loincloths" (Genesis 3:6–7, emphasis added). Think about that for a second. They went from walking around naked without a care in the world to making a decision to put their security in something other than God. In that moment, they went from feeling perfectly secure to instantly insecure, aware of being naked when just a minute earlier, it didn't matter. But then it got worse. The Bible goes on to say that they tried to hide themselves from God. They knew that they had damaged this relationship. Can I just say that making a bad decision to try to feel secure almost always leads to making more bad decisions, which leads to even more insecurity! Adam and Eve tried to hide from God. Think about that. The same God that created everything, including them. Do you really think God didn't know where they were hiding?

Have you ever messed up in a relationship and then tried to avoid that person, hoping it will all go away? I have. When I was in high school, I dented the chrome bumper on our 1970 Dodge Challenger that my grandfather had given us. Fun fact, you can't hide a dent in a large chrome bumper, especially when you back it into a telephone pole. For two weeks, I tried to strategically park it in the driveway to try and hide it from my dad. I was not successful.

Adam and Eve unsuccessfully tried to hide from God. "And they heard the sound of the Lord God walking in the garden in the cool of the day, and the man and his wife hid themselves from the presence of the Lord God among the trees of the garden. But the Lord God called to the man and said to him, 'Where are you?' And he said, 'I heard the sound of you in the garden, and I was afraid, because I was naked, and I hid myself.' He said, 'Who told you that you were naked? Have you eaten of the tree of which I commanded you not to eat?'" (Genesis 3:8–11 ESV). God knew where they were and what they had done. Their relationship with God was forever changed in that one moment. Their best day turned into their worst day, and you and I have been living with the consequences ever since. Now you may be asking, "How in the world could they be so dumb?" They lived in Utopia! They literally hung out with God. They had everything but one suggestion from a serpent, and they chose door number two. Really? As many times as I have heard this story, inevitably someone comes to the conclusion of "How could they be so dumb? They had everything!" Before we pull our judgy pants up too high, let me ask you a question. What's your "piece of fruit"? We all have one. Need some help? What's the thing you try to control so you feel secure? We have a full picture of Eve, so it is easy to judge her actions, but the truth is, we all have that one thing we pursue that we think will provide us with security. If you really want to know the root of our insecurity, it all starts right here. Based on the pattern we talked about in the previous chapter, this is ground zero. Adam and Eve walked with God, felt the pang of insecurity, were tempted (the pivot), and then decided to take control. It brought "temporary security" that ultimately led to unbelievable difficulties, which led to more, almost immediate insecurity. It's something we chose then and something we continue to choose today. God has always wanted something different for us. Allow me to explain.

You and I were created to have a relationship with God. Whether you believe in Him or not, there is something inside of you that identifies with that statement. From the moment we enter this world, mankind is created with a void that can only be satisfied with a relationship with God. It's the source of our security. It hasn't changed since the beginning of time. Oh, we try other things—lots of other things—to fill it, to feel secure. In the end, we are left hopeless. No matter how hard we try, deep down we know that all that "stuff" is temporary. God has always wanted a relationship with mankind—always. In fact, the moment that man decided to blow off God and sin entered the world, God has continued to pursue us. Let that sink into your soul. God is personally pursuing *you*. The world we live in today is not the world God intended for us, which is all the more reason a relationship with Him is so appealing. He knows how to navigate this world.

I know, I know. How could God relate to us? He's God! He can relate to us because He sent His Son, Jesus, to earth. Jesus came to reconcile us to God. We have sin. At the beginning when mankind walked with God, there wasn't any sin. We chose it, and we continue to live with the consequences every single day. Because of sin, we are separated from God. The only way to fix that was to have someone pay for our sin. When someone apologizes for something they have done for you, even though you forgive them, it doesn't change the fact that they did it. We can tell God we are sorry for what we've done but we are still sinners. Only someone who has not sinned can pay for our sin. We can't do it. Jesus was the only One who was without sin. He willingly chose to die on the cross for you and me. Jesus was perfect, and He died for the sins of mankind, and then He rose from the grave. That, my friend, is how much God wants to have a relationship with you and me. But here's the thing, He won't force it on you. It's a gift that you choose. We can't earn it because we don't deserve it, and yet God freely offers it. All you have to do is accept it. It's the only *thing* that can fill the void in our lives. It's what we were created for. Deep down, you know it is true.

Why is this so important? Because as difficult as this world can be, it's temporary. When we die—and we all will—we will stand before God. For those who have accepted God's free gift of salvation that can only come from what Jesus did for us, they will spend eternity with Him in heaven where every day will be perfect. It's the truth. If you decide to reject it, then you chose to spend eternity apart from God...in hell, a place that is absent from the security that only God can give. It is a place of loneliness, torture, and suffering. A place God never intended for mankind. Why is this so important? Because right now, there is a battle in your mind and in your soul. The same "serpent" that whispered in Eve's ear is whispering in yours right now. He knows what hangs in the balance. He knows what a relationship with God can do in your life today right now. Satan knows that true security can only be found in the Creator (God), not in His creation. All of our needs in life can be narrowed down to three categories: the emotional, the physical, and the spiritual.

In the beginning, before sin entered the world, Adam and Eve wanted for nothing. All their physical needs were met. They lived in a harmonious relationship with one another and they lived in a harmonious relationship with God. They trusted Him. The moment they sinned, they needed clothes, they blamed each other for their choice, and they tried to hide from God. How crazy is that?

Now look, I don't want to tell that living in a relationship with God means the absence of trouble. You will still have difficulties in life because we live in a broken world with broken people who do broken things. What it means is that when I am dealing with difficulties in life, I can have peace because I know that God is in control. Read that sentence again. *God is in control.* That's security that only He can provide. It means that God will take care of it, even when I don't understand. It means I don't need to be in control and try to "fix it." How do I know? Because Satan wants you to *think* you can do it on your own, that you can find security in other things, in other ways, until you step out into eternity. He knows that by then, it will be too late. Having a relationship with God is the single most important decision in your life. Security for today, tomorrow, and eternity. It's the missing piece you've been searching for your entire life. God's arms are wide open. Forgiveness and peace are waiting for you. All you have to do is ask, and He does the rest. That, my friend, is how it was always meant to be.

3

My Puffy Chest

There are several animals that are known for getting all puffed up to help them get through life. The frigate bird, for example, has a large red sack on their chest that inflates to the size of a football. Apparently, it's a big hit with the ladies. Howler monkeys, considered one of the loudest animals on land, use air sacs that they inflate to raise the level of their voice. A puffer fish can inflate its entire body to warn predators to back off. If that doesn't do the trick, as a bonus feature they also have poisonous spikes that could kill up to thirty people! But probably my favorite "I get puffy" animal is the male hooded seal found in the Arctic and North Atlantic oceans. They have *two* inflatable sacs on the top of their head. They use it to let other animals know who they are and what they are all about. It's a display of aggression against other males *Back off, man!* and to attract the ladies' attention. *Hey, baby. How you doin'?* The second inflatable sac, and probably my favorite part, is a large pinkish balloon that comes out of the nostril. I'm not making this up. During their mating season, they use it to warn off other males by inflating it and shaking it around. Apparently, a large pink nostril balloon is quite intimidating. Coincidentally, that same nose balloon is rather, shall we say, *attractive* with the ladies.

We humans have our own version of getting puffy. It's called pride. Whether it's to let others know what you are all about, telling people to back off, or to impress the opposite sex, we have developed our own defense mechanisms to gain control of any situation. We may not have a balloon coming out of our nose, but we may scream, use physical force, gossip, drive a flashy car, buy a round of drinks for the table, obsess over the perfect picture for our social media post or… Do I need to go on? I know it seems odd to have a chapter on pride in a book about insecurity, but here's the ugly awful truth—pride and insecurity go hand in hand.

I want to pick at insecurity for a second. At its root, insecurity is a lack of confidence. I feel unsure about something and I need to feel secure, so I reach for control. That's the pivot. I make a decision to do, say, move, or react in a way that will somehow produce a form of security in my life. I know best, or at least I want to think that I know best. In reality, I just want to feel secure about the situation. I'll do what it takes to make that happen. Notice all the "I" statements I just made? Pride writes checks that our emotional bank cannot cover. Remember what I said in chapter 1, every bad decision I have ever made in my life has come out of insecurity. So what is pride, really? I laughed when I looked up the definition.

pride \ˈprīd\ (noun): inordinate self-esteem

Exceeding a reasonable amount of self-esteem. Fake it until you make it. Control it until you feel better. Have you ever been around a prideful person? It's not a good feeling. With my "judgy pants" pulled way up high, I often think, *I wonder what they are hiding.* I'm not talking about someone having confidence. My experience has shown me that people who are confident in something are often quite humble about it. The opposite has also shown me that the louder and more braggadocios a person is about something, the more often they are trying to convince themselves of it as well. Think about the relationship with insecurity and pride, the dance that they do together. We've seen it in others and have probably run a few laps with it ourselves. A boss that uses their position of power over others. Friends who manipulate events so it works out best for them. Spouses who weaponize sex or finances to get what they want. Conversations we have about other people to manipulate the situation to our advantage. Don't even get me started with our online activities. In the version of the story we tell, we make ourselves the hero and them the villain. Maybe that last one was a little too close to home. Pursuing security through insecure means will only get you more insecurity. Pride makes you think that this time it will be different. It's about control. Correction, it's about *perceived* control. We think in the short-term fulfillment instead of the long term consequences. Pride is thinking that I have the solution. Experience has taught me that I don't.

In Isaiah 30:1, the Bible talks about the progression of our insecurity, pride, and control, "'Ah, stubborn children,' declares the Lord, 'who carry out a plan, but not mine, and who make an alliance, but not of my Spirit, that they may add sin to sin.'" Think of the story of Adam and Eve on that fateful day. That's exactly what they did. That's exactly what we still do.

Have you ever gone out to eat and when you asked someone where they want to go, they say they don't care; but then when you pick a place, all they do is complain about it? It shows up innocently enough. Control is me trying to manipulate a situation into an outcome that favors me. It's the woman who unbuttons the extra button to get noticed. It's the person who has to be "in the know." It's trying to show up at a particular spot so your paths just "happen" to cross. Control is a funny word. It's the pinnacle of security, right? I am the king of my castle, the master of my domain. It's all about me.

If you have lived for any length of time, you know that control is temporary. In fact, the longer you've lived, the more you realize how truly temporary it is. Think about some of the bad decisions you have made in your life that in the moment you made them, you thought they were a sure thing. I remember back in 2007, I went in on an investment rental property. At the same time, I also bought a piece of land that I never physically saw in a city I've never been. I was feeling insecure about my financial position and I thought this was the way out. We weren't poor by any means, but we certainly weren't "getting ahead" either. Do you know how easy it is to justify something when you use your own scale of justification?

I was a youth pastor, not making a ton of money, and I was going to help God out with my situation. *Yes, that was an actual stream of consciousness.* I convinced my wife to take equity out of our house to put down on these investments. We couldn't lose. Famous last words. In 2008, the bottom fell out of the housing market. The physical stress and strain it put on our marriage was immense. We were stuck in our "can't lose" investment. Turns out, it was a loser. Now I couldn't have known that the market was going to crash. Life happens. That wasn't the problem. The problem was that I made a rushed decision, focusing on the short-term gains without really considering the long-term exposure to my family. My focus was making a decision for short-term security that was birthed out of insecurity. My pride told me, "You got this." I sought out control, so I took a foolish risk to feel better about my future, and it blew up in my face. It brought me waaay more insecurity than if I had done nothing at all. We got out of the rental house but wound up having to hold on to that worthless piece of dirt for years. We eventually sold it at a giant loss. Pursuing security through insecure means will only get you more insecurity. I have beat myself up for that decision, and many others just like it, for a long, long time. Looking back now, I say to myself, "What were you thinking?" The answer is, I wasn't.

It's weird, but I have found that just before the pivot, in that moment of decision, there is this feeling inside that says you probably shouldn't move forward, call it a moment of conscience. To pursue security through insecure means always involves compromise. Pride has a tendency to give you the courage to push through the compromise. This time will be different. Security is just around the corner.

I'm the one who is in control. It's just a small compromise. Can those two words even exist in the same sentence?

Think back to some of your compromise moments. Running up charges on the credit cards feel great until the bill comes due. Infidelity is fun until your spouse find out. Partying is a blast until you wake up the next morning, wondering what happened the night before. Pornography is exciting until you realize the damage it does to you and to others. Embellishing your credentials feels great until someone verifies your story. It will feel good for a little while. It's temporary. The well-told story of the date we shouldn't have but tell ourselves that it's better than being alone can easily turn into a one-night stand that becomes a pregnancy or STD conversation with the person you will eventually marry. Or perhaps it's the discussion we shouldn't have right now but we must get our point across, that turns into an argument where voices are raised, that leads to win at all costs, that leads to words said in anger that cannot be taken back. *Oh, we showed them!* It's a temporary security that later turns into regret. *I want to feel better* becomes *I should know better* that becomes *What have I done?* This leads an even greater need to feel better. In the end, the same pride that convinced us to compromise to try and gain control becomes regret we use to beat ourselves up over the very decisions we made. Insecurity is a vicious cycle.

Did you know that anger is a secondary emotion? Anger is caused by something else. You are angry because of something or someone. I like to say it this way, anger is a reaction to not getting the results I want. Anger shows up in insecurity. It's wrapped in pride. It is the absence of control, a real emotion with real consequences. I have met lots of angry people, but I have never met someone who enjoys being angry. It's exhausting because there is always a source attached to it. It is the end result of our pride. Every bad decision we've made in our search for security through insecure means ultimately lands us here. Maybe your anger is aimed toward others or maybe your anger is directed toward yourself, but it is definitely a by-product of our insecurity journey. I've spent more than a few nights lying awake in bed, being angry with someone who did something to me or I'm angry at myself for something that I did. So how do we move past it? To answer that question, let's take a quick trip down memory lane. Insecurity is a lack of confidence, and our pride tells us we can feel secure by taking control, which is temporary, that ultimately leads to more insecurity. Quite frankly, that makes us mad. We are going to spend some time talking about regret and forgiveness in a few chapters.

What I want to focus on right now is that if our pride (control) ultimately yields anger, then it is also safe to say that humility (surrender) will bring us peace. Romans 12:3 says, "For by the grace given to me I say to everyone among you not to think of himself more highly than he ought to think, but to think with sober judgment, each according to the measure of faith that God has assigned." Since our source of lasting security can only be found in a relationship with God (see previous chapter), that would mean that we cannot provide our own security. That would also mean we would have to trust that God is in control of everything. Yikes! The ironic thing I find in all of this, allowing God to be in control in my life, is that my pride, the thing that only yields more insecurity, constantly gets in the way of preventing me from having the very thing I have always wanted—security. It's placing trust in God versus trust in myself.

Allow me to go back to my investment example. I made that decision because I was trying to help God make my life better. I was placing myself equal to God. Wow! That is hard to write but it's true. It's the serpent whispering in my ear that God is holding out on me. But what would have happened if at the point of decision (the pivot), I went to God about my decision before I made it. If my original premise was that I needed more money to feel better, then that would mean that wealth would be the source of my security, not God. Since I know that can't be true, it would have caused me to rethink my decision before I made the decision. If I had yielded control and told myself that since God is the source of my security, He knows how much money I make and what I need. He will take care of it. If he wants me to invest in something, He will provide the opportunity. It won't be created (controlled) by me. Wait, so God doesn't want me to be wealthy? That's the wrong question. God doesn't want me to place my security in wealth because it will not satisfy my ultimate desire for security. Also, by placing my trust in God and not making a bad decision out of insecurity, it would have alleviated a lot of stress in my life. My pride fights that.

Have you ever considered that maybe God is protecting you from harm instead of keeping you from good? Staying home, not compromising your standards, and waiting for "Mr. Right" could be more about protecting you from pain than about Him being a kill-joy to your fun. Trying to find security in my relationships, wealth, popularity, where I live, job title, etc., is all about *me* pursuing *me* for my security and all of the decisions I've made to get there. Our pride keeps us from asking the right question. It's not about missing out on fun, it's about protecting us from pain. That's where trust comes into play. There is nothing intrinsically wrong with pursuing things in life, as long as those pursuits aren't for the sake of feeling secure. It's crazy to think that our pride, the thing that we use to try and gain security, is ultimately what keeps us from experiencing the very thing we need and want the most, real security. Let that thought sink in to your soul.

What are you trying to control? Where are you searching for security? How is it working out for you so far? How about we flip the coin over. What would you gain by trusting God for security? How would you sleep at night, knowing that God has your future and your present? There is a battle going on in your mind right now. I have the same battle. This isn't a "one and done Jesus take the wheel" kind of event. This is an everyday thing. This is "The stock market crashed and my retirement is gone!" This is "My coworker is a jerk, and I have to work there five days a week." This is "My marriage ain't doing so well." Jesus said that you will have problems in this world, but then He followed that statement with "Don't sweat it because I have overcome the world." That's security.

That's peace. That's contentment. That's a decision that you and I have to make every day, sometimes multiple times a day. To realize and to rest in the long-term security of God. We have done it our way for long enough. What have you got to lose? Oh, wait! That's the wrong question. If you lay down your pride, what do you have to gain?

4

Living Securely

What did you want to be when you grew up? Was it a fireman? Perhaps a doctor? Little kids have big dreams. How did yours turn out?

When I was a kid, I wanted to be a professional singer. This was back in the day before reality TV contests and social media accounts. Yes, such a world did exist. I'm the youngest of four, and from the moment I could use words, I was singing. I used to sit in the back of the car, the very back with the backward-facing seat, bouncing back and forth and just making up songs. I drove my siblings crazy. I used to sit in my room, listening to records *oh, man, do I sound old* and make up dance moves. Oh yes, dance moves. As I got older, it turned out I actually had a bit of talent with the ol' vocal pipes. The dancing, not so much. I began to enter talent competitions, and to my surprise, I would win. I remember when I was around eight years old when I won first place in a fine arts contest. There just happened to be a talent agent sitting in the audience that evening. He approached my parents and told them I needed to go to the city of Boston to get more noticed. I remember having a conversation with my parents a few days later. They decided I was too young. I believe that was a "fork in the road" moment for me. Who knows what would have happened to me if my parents had gone the other direction. Perhaps

I would have joined a boy band, maybe even the one that came out of the Boston area *oh, oh, oh oooh, oh, the right...* Perhaps I should let that one go.

I still pursued singing. I still wanted to be rich and famous, performing on a large stage, belting out magical tunes. I still had the dream. Let me tell you what wasn't part of the dream—becoming a pastor. Have you ever met a kid who says that when they grow up, they want to be a pastor in a church? Me neither. Yet here I am today, a pastor in a church. You want to know the funny part... This is what I am supposed to be doing with my life. Something I never would have chosen on my own. This calling allowed me to meet my wife, who just happened to live on the other side of the country, have two wonderful kids, and live an incredible life. Have I ever questioned if I should be pastor? Oh yes, yes, I have, but even at the half century point of my life, I can see how God had it planned for me all along.

Now why am I telling you this story? Because depending on your view of God, the words you will read over the next several pages may seem a little far-fetched. Living in a secure relationship with God could easily sound like a fairy tale, something weak people believe in because...well, they are weak. But what if all of the searching in your life came down to this moment?

One of my favorite verses in the Bible is found in John 10:10. Jesus said, "The thief comes only to steal and kill and destroy. I came that they may have life and have it abundantly." What I find so cool about this statement is that Jesus is describing the difference between Him and Satan (the serpent in the garden). Satan wants to ruin your life. Period. End of story. Jesus said that He came to give us life, salvation, the relationship we were always meant to have that we talked about in chapter 2. Now that alone is enough, but Jesus takes it one step further. He says that we can have "life abundantly." I know, I know, *whoopee!* It suddenly sounds like a late night-infomercial, "But wait, there's more!" Some of the English words used in our Bibles today that are translated from the original Greek text fail to capture the rich description of the original word. When you read "abundant," you most likely conclude that it's enough with maybe some left over. In the original Greek text, the word is *perissos*, which means "more than expected, overflowing, special advantage, or beyond the norm." It is overwhelming. Think of it this way. You are thirsty and get a drink from a hose, but that hose is a firehose from a firetruck on full blast. Starting to see the picture? The abundant life, a personal relationship with God, is more than you could hope to have. That life, that relationship, is what you and I can have with God right now. Let that sink in for a moment. *A personal relationship with God.* Jesus didn't just come to die for our sin and rise from dead just so we can go to heaven. That was the beginning, not the end. To have a relationship with God isn't a one and done type of event. Just like getting married isn't a vow and "I'll see you around." Jesus came to restore our broken relationship with God, the Creator of the universe. That's a relationship we can live in right now. That's the "abundant life" He was talking about a real, more than you can imagine, every moment relationship with God. How's that for security! Let me say it this way, Jesus came to provide the security you have always wanted and always needed. Because of Jesus, you can live in that security every single moment of your life.

I'm not a big fan of spiders and I'm not proud to admit it. There has been more than a few times I have hit a rather high note when coming across a spider. Thankfully, my wife does not share the same concerns about spiders in our home. What causes fear in your heart? Is it heights? Public speaking? Perhaps snakes? We all have things that cause fear in our hearts. It's a normal reaction to things we don't prefer. Reacting *to* fear and reacting *out of* fear are two very different things. Screaming like a little girl at the sight of a spider, *I've heard people do that*, versus burning the house to the ground because of said spider would be two very different approaches to the same problem. One is a reaction to fear when I see the spider; the other is reacting out of fear when I burn the house to the ground to kill the same spider. The fear is still there, but the reaction is quite different. Have you ever noticed that you don't have the same fear to everything in your life? I have a friend who is afraid of heights, but I have no problem walking on a suspension bridge. I do have a tingle in my stomach when I look down, but it doesn't cause the same reaction in me as it does in my friend. There are things in all of our lives that are triggers, things that cause fear. How we view that fear will dictate our reaction. If you are fearful of being alone, you will make decisions to ensure that you are with someone, regardless if that is best for your life. The person who is afraid of being poor will handle money differently than the person who is not. If you are afraid of going unnoticed or being disrespected, there are definitely things you can do to make sure that doesn't happen. We are all afraid of something, and I'm not talking about spiders anymore. What is that thing or things that keep you awake at night, the thing that drives you? What would your life look like if you weren't afraid anymore? Have you even considered the possibility?

It is possible to live securely in an insecure world. Let me say that again. It is absolutely possible to live securely in an insecure world. Living in that security doesn't mean that you wake up every day without a care in the world. It means you have peace in the midst of it because of the source of your security. Security is the opposite of fear, but not the absence of fear. It's the difference between fact and fiction. Let me give you an example. In 2008, the stock market took a historic plunge. Many people lost their savings, their retirement, and their hope. Imagine if you were planning on retiring at the end of 2007. You've worked hard your whole life. You've saved. You've planned. Then in one fell swoop, it's all gone. That would cause fear, right? If your security was tied up in your finances and your golden parachute, it would cause downright panic!

Let's take a different perspective for a moment. What if my security rested in God and not my finances? Would I still experience some fear? Probably. Would I stay there? No. Here's why. If I trusted God to handle the finances when I had them, then I can trust God to handle them when I don't have them. My security isn't in the finances, it's in the One who provided them. Follow me on this.

Adam and Eve weren't secure because they looked around and said, "Oh yeah, we are living large!" God provided all they had, all that they saw, and all that they experienced. They lived in relationship with God, and out of that relationship came the blessings from security. I remember 2008. I did panic. I didn't rest in my relationship with God. I made some foolish decisions because I thought it was all on me. I tried to control my security and failed miserably. Even though I could have rested in God, I chose to react in panic. God was there, but I chose to go a different path. Fast forward to 2020. The stock market took another giant fall. We, along with many others, watched our savings and retirement account drop. I felt the pang of fear, sure, but this time I chose to rest in my relationship with God and the security only He can provide. It was almost the turning of a page. I'm realizing that I either rely on God for everything or I rely on Him for nothing. Personally, option B hasn't turned out too well for me. Do I hope the stock market goes back up, you bet! As I write these words, the market is still on a crazy roller-coaster ride, but I know that ultimately, God will take care of it. If the money comes back, great, but if God chooses a different path for me and my family, that's okay too. I mean that today, I paid lip service to it in 2008. The same can be said about relationships, where you work, family dynamics, etc. Whatever the circumstance, if your security rests on you and your control, you are in for a bumpy ride that will most certainly end in greater insecurity.

Living in security in our relationship with God does not mean our world is perfect and easy. Not at all. Jesus told us so in Matthew 5:45, "For he makes his sun rise on the evil and on the good, and sends rain on the just and on the unjust." In John 16:33, Jesus said, "I have said these things to you, that in me you may have peace. In the world you will have tribulation. But take heart; I have overcome the world." Read that verse again. Jesus tells us first that in Him we find peace because bad things will happen, *but* don't worry. He's bigger than what happens here in the world. A relationship with God through Jesus isn't the absence of trouble, it's security in Him when you go through it. All of us will go through something. We live in a broken world with broken people who do broken things. If my security is found in anything other than God, eventually that "thing" will let me down. Why? Because it cannot provide lasting security. You know it. You've experienced it. When I talk about living in security with God it doesn't mean my friends won't let me down, my finances will be there, or I live to a ripe old healthy age. If anyone tells you there's another way, they are probably selling something. I don't need control to be content. I don't need to prove something to have value. True peace and contentment can only be found in God. That's what you get from living securely in a relationship with Him. That's the abundant life. It's not the trouble-free life, but a life of security when bad things happen.

We struggle with this truth because it means we have to move from my control to God's control. My experience is that He tends to view the world differently than I do. That's a good thing. That's a very good thing. Everybody needs an "Attaboy!" or "Attagirl!" every once in a while. There is something about knowing a person is in your corner, that they have your back. We all need that. Do you believe that God is *for* you? Honestly, do you believe that God is for *you*? That may sound like a dumb question, but I believe it is a giant stumbling block for people. Do you think that God is only for you as long as you "do good"? Take one step out of line and *whamo!* God will smite you. I used to think that way. I lived in fear of God. It's hard to feel secure about God when you think you are one step away from His wrath. I realize that humility isn't a bad thing. Remember, we are sinners. We bring nothing to the table. That's why our relationship with God is about God doing all the work to provide the gift of salvation. We can't get to Him; He comes to us. I used to think He did it out of obligation, not out of love. I didn't know how to enjoy a relationship with Him. I think that is part of our insecurity. How could God want a relationship with me? Sometimes I don't even want a relationship with me. May I share something with you that you may not have heard before?

> *He brought me out into a broad place; he res-*
> *cued me, because he delighted in me.* (Psalm 18:19)

The LORD your God is in your midst, a mighty one who will save; he will rejoice over you with gladness; he will quiet you by his love; he will exult over you with loud singing. (Zephaniah 3:17)

For I, the LORD your God, hold your right hand; it is I who say to you, "Fear not, I am the one who helps you." (Isaiah 41:13)

Out of my distress I called on the LORD; the LORD answered me and set me free. The LORD is on my side; I will not fear. What can man do to me? (Psalm 118:5–6)

I sought the LORD, and he answered me and delivered me from all my fears. (Psalm 34:4)

This I know, that God is for me. (Psalm 56:9)

God is for you. God, the Creator of the universe—who sent His only Son Jesus to pay for your sins, who wants so much to live in relationship with you, who is for...you. When you can begin to lean into that, when you can learn to live in that, your view of your life and the world in which you live begins to look very different. You can trust that God wants what is best for you. You can rest in Him. You can have peace in the midst of difficulty. You can be content instead of being afraid. You can live in the security of God the way you were meant to live from the very beginning.

Somewhere along the way, we've been told that if we begin a relationship with God, then life will be boring. We will have to go to church every day and become a missionary to some unknown group of people or community group on the back side of nowhere. We will be poor and walk around in hand-me-down clothes. A life with God is no life at all. Where do you think that narrative started?

> *But the serpent said to the woman, "You will not surely die. For God knows that when you eat of it your eyes will be opened, and you will be like God, knowing good and evil." (Genesis 3:4–5)*

Satan has been lying to us since the beginning. He continues to lie to us in this very moment. He knows that living securely in our relationship with God is what we need. He's always known it. I think we have too. God is for me. God wants what is best for me. God says it this way, "Cease *striving* and know that I am God…" (Psalm 46:10 NASB1995). It's not a fairy tale, it's a truth you can rely on. It's our security.

I started this chapter by telling you about the plans I had for my life. The bright lights of the big stage and all that it would have provided would have been fun, but for my life, it would have been "second best." Quite honestly, it could have very easily been a disaster for me. I can look back now and see how being a pastor was always God's best for me. I wouldn't have chosen it but honestly, I wouldn't have changed it either. The road hasn't always been easy. Some of that was self-inflicted; some of it was inflicted by others. All of it brought me to this point of being able to say to you that my security comes from my relationship with God. He is for me, He delights in me, and His plan for my life is best. The same is true for you.

5

The Spiritual Side of Insecurity

As I said earlier, I love a good conversation. More to the point, I love to hear people's stories. One of my favorite questions to ask is, "If you could replay one moment in your life exactly as it happened, what would it be?" I have been able to hear more stories through that one simple question. We all have memories, and it is fun to recount the good ones—a wedding day, the birth of a child, a promotion at work, or purchasing your first car. It's good to be able to share them with others. It connects us. I have found something interesting in asking this question, and I'm guessing that when I ask you, the same will be true as well. Recounting the *good moment* may take some effort, but inevitably, there is something to share. Watch what happens when we flip the question around just a bit. What is a moment in your life that you wish you change? Almost instantly, something pops in your head. Why is that? Why is it harder to come up with the good stories than it is to recount a bad one?

We all live with regret. For some of us, it seems like an insurmountable mountain that is always in full view. *Hello, insecurity! I've missed you.* I have played more than one scenario in my head of how I wished I had done something different, gone somewhere different, walked away, kept my mouth shut, or never met that person. Are you with me? The ugly truth is that we wallow in it because we can't change it. The deep well we jumped into has slippery walls that prevent us from climbing out. I think for many of us, this is the vicious cycle that we keep repeating in our minds, maybe even in our lives. We seem to self-sabotage, eventually giving up hope that it will get better, that we will get better. Do you remember when we talked about Adam and Eve and how the serpent whispered in their ear that God was holding out on them and how much better life would be on their own? Then they acted out of their insecurity to pursue a false sense of security, and we know how that turned out. Have you ever thought about what Satan whispered in their ear that first night they tried to sleep? "You just ruined mankind." "God hates you." "You are such a disappointment." "You can never be loved." "You will never recover from this." "Your life is over." Talk about regret! I can't even imagine what that was like for them…or can I? Come to think of it, I've had those same thoughts. I've arrived at those very same conclusions. I've believed those very same things. How can that be? I mean, God was sad, and there were consequences for their actions, but nowhere do I read that God stopped loving them. Nowhere does it say that they were beyond the reach of God. He was still there.

Where does regret come from? I don't mean how we arrive at regret, I've got that part nailed down. I mean regret itself. *Regret* is defined as "sorrow aroused by circumstances beyond one's control or power to repair." It isn't a word we think about in the moment. In the moment, we are just euphoric about being on top, winning the day. Regret comes later when we come down from the high. I find it odd that I don't really consider regret when I'm acting out of my insecurity, even though I've experienced it many, many times. If our security comes from God and regret is a by-product or a result of us acting out of our insecurity, then can we agree that regret comes from Satan? Just follow my train of thought for a second. He promised the world to Adam and Eve, knowing it was going to end in disaster, and then he beat them up over their self-centered stupidity. Let me pull the covers back a little bit because Satan has been portrayed as this mischievous little guy who sits on your shoulder and coaxes you into making bad decisions. The devil made me do it, right? As much as God loves you and wants a personal relationship with you, Satan hates you and wants to destroy your life. Furthermore, he knows what waits beyond the grave. He knows his days are numbered, and he knows he will spend eternity in hell, tormented forever. Guess what? He wants to take you with him.

> *Because they exchanged the truth about God for a lie and worshiped and served the creature rather than the Creator, who is blessed forever! Amen.* (Romans 1:25)

> *Be sober-minded; be watchful. Your adversary the devil prowls around like a roaring lion, seeking someone to devour.* (1 Peter 5:8)

> *For though we walk in the flesh, we are not waging war according to the flesh. For the weapons of our warfare are not of the flesh but have divine power to destroy strongholds. We destroy arguments and every lofty opinion raised against the knowledge of God, and take every thought captive to obey Christ.* (2 Corinthians 10:3–5)

Satan knows how this all turns out, just like he knows you will regret the decisions you make, trying to pursue your own security. This is his plan, and he has been doing it since the very beginning of our existence. Now here is the real ugly truth. The devil doesn't make you do it, we do it to ourselves. May I digress for just a moment? Too often God gets blamed for the stupidity of man. We choose sin, we choose our own path, and then when our bad decisions blow up in our face, somehow it's God's fault. We've been blaming God for our decisions since the very beginning. Adam told God that the woman He created gave him the fruit. We need to put on our big boy and big girl pants and own our decisions. Satan didn't grab Eve's hand, pick the fruit, and then shove it down her throat. She chose to do it. So do we. Why is that important? Because we can also choose not to give in to our insecurity. It is easy? Not always, especially in the beginning. Sin makes all kinds of promises without revealing the true cost until it's too late. Satan knows that the source of our security can only come from God. Since he wants to destroy our lives, he is going to promise anything and everything to keep us from it. In John 8:48, Jesus calls him the "father of lies." To recap, Satan wants to destroy your life and will say anything to convince you to do it. If we were to end the chapter here, that would be pretty depressing. Live with your regret. Good luck to you. Well just as much as Satan wants to destroy us, God wants to restore us. Even when we blow Him off, even when we are living with regret, Jesus tells us there is a better way.

> *"Come to me, all who labor and are heavy laden, and I will give you rest. Take my yoke upon you, and learn from me, for I am gentle and lowly in heart, and you will find rest for your souls. For my yoke is easy, and my burden is light."* (Matthew 11:28–30)

Satan offers regret. Jesus offers rest. And not just physical rest, but rest for your soul. That place way down deep where we house our regret. Jesus doesn't come and smack us upside the head, rub our nose in it, tell us all about our stupidity. Actually he does just the opposite. He invites us into relationship. He understands. He offers healing. But it isn't forced, we have to choose.

> *For we do not have a high priest who is unable to sympathize with our weaknesses, but one who in every respect has been tempted as we are, yet without sin. Let us then with confidence draw near to the throne of grace, that we may receive mercy and find grace to help in time of need.* (Hebrews 4:15–16)

Mercy, grace, and help—that's what Jesus is offering. One of my favorite books is *He Loves Me!* by Wayne Jacobsen. It is a book I highly recommend. Outside of the Bible, it has be one of the most influential sources in shaping how I see God. If you are unfamiliar with the rest of the story of Adam and Eve, after they sin, God passes judgment for their choices. It is the consequences of their decisions. God removes them from the garden of Eden. He removes them from paradise. I've always read that as the heavy hand of God's judgment, the "wrath of God!" In some respect, that is true. Do you also know that God was showing love to them as well? In the book, Wayne talks about some of the other aspects of the garden. There was this other tree that God created, the tree of life. Wayne concludes that because God loved Adam and Eve, He needed to remove them from the tree of life because they would continue to live in their sinful nature and be separated from Him forever. The Bible doesn't say exactly what the tree of life provided, but let's say for sake of argument that it meant they would never die if they ate it. Because of their sin and what it did to creation, they would live in a sinful world with sinful bodies forever. God loved them so much and wanted to be reconciled with them, so He removed them from the garden. It was both love and consequences.

Think of it this way. If my daughter burned her hand on the hot stove and I no longer allowed her around the stove, would you conclude that I did that out of love or out of anger? Wayne's perspective on this story caused me to see God in a completely different way. Some of you have walked away from God. Somehow, He let you down. He didn't come through the way you thought it should have gone down. You may have given up on God, but He has continued to be near you, no matter what you have done. You are not too broken for God to heal. Are there consequences for our actions? Absolutely. As much as I don't want my daughter to burn her hand on the stove, if she chooses to touch it, she will feel the consequences of her decision. That doesn't change how much I love her nor does it prevent me from coming to her aid, putting ointment on her burn, and hold her while she cries. God wants to do the same thing for you and me. You and I cannot fix our past. Only God can do that. So what do I do with my regret? How do I move past it?

I have a confession to make. There are times when I enjoy witty sarcasm. When I was in the early years of ministry, there was a trend to put up motivational posters that had one word with an inspirational quote after it. Things like *teamwork, integrity,* and *confidence* would grace the walls of many offices. I had one in mine. One day, I can across this website that made demotivational posters, and they are hilarious. One that sticks out is a picture of a partially sunken ship that says, "Mistakes. It could be that the purpose of your life is only to serve as a warning to others." I know, I know, I shouldn't laugh. The poster sort of encapsulates our feelings of regret. The best I can do with my mistakes is warn others not to repeat them. That is partially true, but I believe that there is something greater in them. First, let me state that everyone has regrets. Everyone. We have a tendency to believe the whisper that we are all alone, and that is a lie.

> *"But watch yourselves lest your hearts be weighed down with dissipation and drunkenness and cares of this life, and that day come upon you suddenly like a trap. 35 For it will come upon all who dwell on the face of the whole earth."* (Luke 21:34–35)

We also believe that we will never get past *it*, that we are doomed to repeat it. That is also a lie. The choice we made to make the bad decision is the same choice we make to move past it.

> *Do not be anxious about anything, but in everything by prayer and supplication with thanksgiving let your requests be made known to God. And the peace of God, which surpasses all understanding, will guard your hearts and your minds in Christ Jesus. Finally, brothers, whatever is true, whatever is honorable, whatever is just, whatever is pure, whatever is lovely, whatever is commendable, if there is any excellence, if there is anything worthy of praise, think about these things.* (Philippians 4:6–8)

I'm not saying we just have to suck it up and move forward. What I am saying is this, have you made things right God? Have you acknowledged you sinned and asked for forgiveness? If the regret you carry involves someone else, have you asked them for forgiveness? By the way, that includes forgiving yourself. If the answer to those questions is "yes," then the person bringing it back up in your mind isn't God.

As far as the east is from the west, so far does he remove our transgressions from us. (Psalm 103:12)

I, I am he who blots out your transgressions for my own sake, and I will not remember your sins. (Isaiah 43:25)

God wants us to live in relationship with Him. He has provided a way for us to do that. The Bible isn't a list of rules and regulations to control us. It is God's guidelines to help us. He knows the best way for us to navigate this broken world. When we blow it and do our own thing, acknowledge it and make things right with Him. That's the end of it. God doesn't keep rubbing our nose in it. So when we go down the memory lane of regret, we need to remind ourselves that we have asked God for His forgiveness and then choose to live in that forgiveness. God's forgiveness is not the absence of consequences. Adam and Eve were still removed from the garden. They still lived in a broken world, but God didn't continue to shame them. He wants a restored relationship with us. Can good things come out of our sin? Why, yes. Yes, they can.

And we know that for those who love God all things work together for good, for those who are called according to his purpose. (Romans 8:28)

I recently had a conversation with a friend of mine about parenting. My kids are older now, but his are coming up the ranks. I was able to share with him some of the things I have learned from doing it wrong, like the times when I puffed out my chest and said things to my kids out of insecurity because I wanted them to know that I was the dad! I wanted him to avoid the pain and embarrassment that my kids and I experienced. There have been bad decisions that I have made that God, in His kindness, brought something good out of them in my life.

Remember the story I told you about borrowing money against my mortgage and how awesome that turned out. That regret followed me for years and years. I felt like such a failure. Fast forward to 2012 when we moved to Washington from California. The housing market was just starting to recover. When we sold our house, we barely broke even. We lost all the equity in our house. I kept thinking about my stupidity and how I had let my wife and kids down. When we moved to Washington, we found a house but had no money to put down so we had to do some creative financing. The loan we got took longer to get approved, which meant we had to wait. Well, it just so happened that there was an older couple in our new church that allowed me and my family (animals too) to live with them for what we thought would be a very short period of time. It turned into almost two months. Here we were, away from family in a new state, sponging off the kindness of strangers because of my stupidity years ago. What happened next was something that only God could have done. We began building a relationship with this couple. We had to do some work on our new house that kept my wife and me away. My kids began building a deep relationship with this couple. They went from friends to family. We began to share birthdays and holidays. They attended sporting events. Our kids introduced *High School Musical* to them, and they liked it. Our lives began to intersect on a regular basis. Fast forward a few Christmases when my girls gave them the present of picking out their "grandparent names." I'm tearing up right now writing this down. This couple is now officially called Nana and Papa. They are the third set of grandparents. They refer to my girls as their granddaughters even as they now enter their adult years. Someday they will be invited to the weddings. Someday they will get pictures of the great grandkids. They are family to us.

Why is this story so important to me? God took a foolish mistake that I made and turned into a blessing for me and my family. If we had the money to put down on the house when we moved to Washington, we probably wouldn't have stayed with them so long. I'm not saying they wouldn't be a part of our lives today, but the fact that we had to live with them was a blessing in so many ways. It has taken some time for me to see the good that God made in my life. Perhaps if you look around, you may just see some of it in your situation as well. God can take our regrets and turn them into blessings. Only God can do that. I am living proof. Perhaps by sharing my story with you, it is part of the good as well.

When we keep living in the past, a past we can't change, a past that breeds even more insecurity, it can easily drive us away from God. We cycle back to taking control and trying to rewrite our history. In the end, we know it doesn't work. Running from God and blaming God isn't the answer. In fact, it just keeps us from the One who is the answer. When you and I rest in the source of security, our relationship with God, we can learn to move past our regrets, because that is the blessing of God's security. Have you walked away from God? He is still there beside you. Are you ready to put down the personal punching bag? He is here to heal your wounds. We don't have to live in our regrets anymore. It's time to let them go and move forward. You get to choose. Live in the security of God.

And the peace of God, which surpasses all understanding, will guard your hearts and your minds in Christ Jesus. (Philippians 4:7)

6

Forgiving Securely

Sometimes people are just jerks. I know that sounds direct, but it doesn't make it any less true. Insecurity can really bring out the worst in all of us, intentionally or not. We live in a broken world with broken people who do broken things. Maybe it is a bad boss, a coworker, a friend, a spouse, or even a family member, but the chances are pretty good that you have been on the receiving end of someone working out their issues. What do you do with that? Sometimes we can get right down there in the mud and give as good as we get. Sometimes we just sit there and take it. No matter how it plays out, we take a little piece of their insecurity with us when we walk away. Left unresolved, the wound can easily fester into a grudge.

Let's be honest, there are people in this world that we would rather not see again for a while or maybe ever. Have you had that conversation in your head when your paths finally do cross and you are on equal footing? Your well-thought-out response is brilliant. They crumble under your witty intellect. In the end, you have told them what's what, and they have no response except to beg for your forgiveness. Yeah, I've done it too.

As long as we are being honest, this is not a chapter I thought I would ever put to paper. I've had some pretty heinous things done to me. I've been wounded deeply by people who should have known better. I've held on to things longer than I should and have most certainly withheld the very forgiveness that I have asked from others when I have blown it. Sometimes people are jerks. This is a journey that is rather fresh in my life. By writing it, I feel more like a beggar showing other beggars where to find bread than someone who has it all figured out. I don't, but I'm definitely failing forward. It may be one day or sometimes one moment at a time, but it is definitely forward progress. Forgiveness is this universal thing we all want from others we have wronged but find it difficult to give when the offense is on the other person. Some might call that hypocritical. I think they are right. If you and I are to live in the security of our relationship with God, then that means in all areas of our lives, especially this one.

> *Bearing with one another and, if one has a complaint against another, forgiving each other; as the Lord has forgiven you, so you also must forgive. And above all these put on love, which binds everything together in perfect harmony.* (Colossians 3:13–14)

In 2019, at the ripe young age of forty-nine, I got my first tattoo. Yup, I got some street cred ink on my arm. It is a verse I came across a few years back when I was going through a rather difficult period in my life. I had been wounded deeply and seriously considered getting out of ministry altogether. I find it interesting how God meets us in some of the darkest and lowest points in our lives. It shouldn't surprise me. This verse helped me turn a corner and pushed me to write this book. It is a constant reminder when I want to pivot and take control that my security, regardless of the circumstances, can only be found in God. Here is what it says.

> *The Lord will fight for you, and you have only to be silent.* (Exodus 14:14)

I remember the first time I read that verse. I wasn't sure I could trust it to be true. I mean, I know it is true because I believe what the Bible says is true, but I struggled to believe it because there is the right way and Kevin's way to handle a situation. Quite frankly, I want my own way, thank you very much. In my own insecurity, I have often felt the need to stand up for myself, especially when I feel misunderstood—*especially* when I feel attacked. Oh, man! You want to talk about control and then struggling to let it go? Ladies and gentlemen, I am exhibit A. See here was my problem, if I didn't stand up for myself, who will? The answer, it turns out, is God, and He is much better at it than I will ever be.

This verse comes out of a very well-known story in the Old Testament. Israel had just been released from their Egyptian slavery by Pharaoh after God had sent plague after plague upon Egypt. By the way, this wasn't a small band of brothers, this was the entire nation of Israel. Imagine a large metropolitan city of roughly a million people just decided one morning to leave the city and head out of town, led by one man—let's call him Moses. Now imagine it's out in the desert. To add some excitement, Pharaoh had a change of heart and decided he liked having them as slaves so he sent out his army to get them back. Here is Israel trekking through the desert with the Red Sea in front of them and a giant army in pursuit. Needless to say, they were a little stressed. The Bible says that the people started freaking out and complaining to Moses about their lives being over and how terrible he was for leading them out here and where is God when you need Him… Get the picture? Moses knew that God was the One who was leading them and that God would take care of them. Isn't it a beautiful thing to watch someone lead out of their security in God? Listen to Moses' response to the Israelites:

> *And Moses said to the people, "Fear not, stand firm, and see the salvation of the Lord, which he will work for you today. For the Egyptians whom you see today, you shall never see again.* **The Lord**

**will fight for you, and you have only to be
silent.**" (Exodus 14:13–14, emphasis added)

Moses knew that God had it covered. What happened next was
a miracle. God tells Moses to stretch out his staff over the water, and
then God parts the Red Sea. The entire nation of Israel walks across
on *dry land!* When they get to the other side, God closes the sea.
Pharaoh's army drowns. Israel is safe. God did what only God can do.

What does that have to do with holding a grudge toward someone? Well, everything, especially if the wounds go deep and wide,
like an ocean. Often we don't want to forgive or release someone
of an offense because if we do, they get away with it. There is no
payment for the wrong that was done to us. We demand justice.
We want our pound of flesh, and we want it now. By holding an
offense over someone, I have a false sense of control. Notice I said
"false sense." Often the person doesn't know we are mad. Or if they
do, they don't care. It is like eating rat poison and then staring at the
rat, hoping it will die. That is what it is like holding on to a grudge.
The only person it hurts is you. I know we want them to apologize,
to admit they were wrong, and to own the pain they put in our lives.
In a weird way, our attempt to control the situation by demanding
something from them is actually giving them more control in our
lives. In a perfect world, everyone would acknowledge their faults
and make things right when they hurt someone. We don't live in a
perfect world. Ugh!

By now, you may be steaming inside. Reading this chapter has
brought to the surface some very ugly memories attached to some
even uglier feelings. Let me ask you something. Where is your security? Is it in the apology? Is it vengeance? Yes, people need to apologize and ask for forgiveness, I agree. That is true in my life when I
blow it, and it is true in yours when you offend. But where is your
security? Is it in the apology or is it in God? If the security comes
from them clearing the ledger, then perhaps it is more about being
in control and less about restoration. I stand on my "rightness," not

in God's righteousness. My security doesn't come from whether they makes thing right or not. My security comes from God, knowing that He will handle it. He wants His best for me and them. He wants to work in my life and in their life. It is difficult for me to accept that God is for me *and* for them. Here is something that God has been teaching me in my journey. I need to trust that God will stand up for me because God is writing all of our stories, not just mine.

Allow me to explain. I am a pastor in a medium-sized town but in a large church. There are lots of people who know me, but I don't necessarily know them. Let's say that I am in a store and a person from church sees me down an aisle and waves to me, but I don't see them so I don't wave back. Then let's say that this person gets offended and is mad that one of their pastors didn't say hello to them. Then for kicks and giggles, let's say that some time passes, and this person tells me about the "blow-off incident" that I didn't even know had taken place. During our conversation, the person learns that I was in the middle of an emergency at home and had to find a specific item in the store and get home as quickly as I could. Do you think they would understand my response in the store with more clarity? No, of course not. Sometimes people are jerks, remember? I'm kidding. Yes, of course a reasonable person with some clarifying information would be inclined to offer more grace. That is what God is asking us to do. I don't know what God is doing in your story, but I do know that God is constantly working in our lives.

We all have blind spots, and we need to trust that God sees them better in other people than we do. Perhaps you should read that last sentence again. We don't know what is happening in their lives. We don't know what God is doing. Perhaps you are experiencing the blowback from their insecurity. Perhaps they are pushing God away, and you are feeling the effects of it. The truth is, we don't know. Does it excuse their behavior? Absolutely not! It does, however, give us clarity. God is writing all of our stories. When I continue to hold an offense over someone, to withhold forgiveness from them, I am telling God how to write their chapter. God, don't you see what they did to me? *Hello, control!* Who am I to tell God how to do anything? Living securely in my relationship with God means that God will take my offense. He will handle it. Does it mean that I can never stand up for myself? No, of course not, but I better check my heart when I do it. The Bible has a lot to say about that. Does it mean that I keep being an emotional punching bag? No, I believe it is wise to have boundaries as long as I don't weaponize them. Guilty as charged. There have been times that my "boundaries" are just a nice way of saying, "I'm still holding a grudge." I'm still working on this one. It's about control or, more to the point, about releasing control and letting God handle it. Then, and only then, will you start to feel better. Only then will you start to heal.

God has a sense of humor. Don't let anyone tell you different. God has a plan for our lives, and it is a very good plan. Do you want to know how God wants us to move forward? Kindness.

> *Let love be genuine. Abhor what is evil; hold fast to what is good. Love one another with brotherly affection. Outdo one another in showing honor.* (Romans 12:9–10)

> *Do not be overcome by evil, but overcome evil with good.* (Romans 12:21)

Now this part can get a little tricky because in our insecurity, we can try to get someone to "like" us so we feel secure. In other words, we can easily come back for more from the very people that will continue to hurt us. This chapter isn't about boundaries, although I'm a huge believer in them. I highly recommend the books *Boundaries* by Henry Cloud and John Townsend and *Love Like You've Never Been Hurt* by Jentezen Franklin. Two great resources that go way deeper on a subject we are covering in one chapter.

How do you love someone securely that has done you wrong? Especially someone that hasn't made it right and probably never will.

You do it securely from your relationship with God. You do it in His power. You do it through the power of Christ. You do it through the Holy Spirit that lives inside of you. I can be kind to someone who is unkind. Jesus did it all the time. I can love someone who is unlovable. Jesus hung out with the worst in society and was even mocked for doing it. I can forgive someone who hasn't asked for it. As He was dying on the cross, Jesus asked God to forgive the very people who had just beaten, tortured, and nailed Him to that very same cross. I can release an offense because my security doesn't come from a pound of flesh. It comes from the love that Christ showed me when He chose to die for my sins. I place the responsibility in God's Hands to deal with that person in a way that will bring him or her restoration with God. Ultimately, that is the goal for all of us. I don't do it out of arrogance, like somehow I am better than them. I don't do it out of pity, as if this poor person doesn't quite have it all figured out. I do it out of humility as someone who has hurt others, both intentionally and unintentionally. I do it as someone who needs forgiveness from God every day. I can release an offense because God does the same for me. God knows the damage it will do in my life by holding on to something I was never meant to hold. He loves me enough to ask me to let it go. To place it in His Hands. That is one of the many benefits of living securely in my relationship with God.

So what is your Red Sea? Maybe your spouse cheated on you. Perhaps someone was spreading gossip about you, trying to ruin your reputation or a bad work environment. Maybe it is family wounds, a sexual assault, or physical abuse. No one goes through life pain free. Who do you need to forgive? What grudge are you holding over someone's head? How has that been working for you so far? God will fight for you in ways you can't even begin to imagine. He is working in all of our lives. Will you trust Him enough to do it? Forgiving securely out of relationship with God isn't easy, but it is what is best. You were not meant to walk through this life with the burden of resentment. I know it seems insurmountable. Perhaps the person you need to forgive first is yourself. Maybe you need to let go of the things we talked about in the last chapter. By withholding forgiveness for yourself, you are trying to hold a standard even God doesn't place on you.

Have you made things right with God and sought His forgiveness? Accept it. When you are reminded of your past, know that it isn't God who is bringing it up. The same holds true for those who have wronged you. Forgive and move forward. Let it go. Let them go. Does it mean they just get a *pass*? I don't know the answer to that. Trusting God means I trust Him with all of it. I know that God is working in my life just like I know He is working in their life. I can't fix them any more than someone can fix me. Only God has the ability to do that. My way would end in disaster because I would try to be in control. Trust that God will take care of it. Forgiving securely out of our relationship with God is a process. It takes time. Franklin Jentezen calls them mile markers that someday you will look back on and reflect how far God has moved you forward from that moment in your life.

I'm learning to live like this. This chapter is part of that process. I've had a few epiphanies while writing it. There are always going to be difficult people in this world, some might even call them *jerks*. I don't know why they are acting that way. I am only responsible for my side of the fence. Are there times that I still want my pound of flesh—to right the wrongs of my past and defend my honor, you bet. But these days, I'm learning to live in the security of God's forgiveness and the power it has not only in my life, but the lives of those around me as well. God is writing all of our stories. I don't need to have all the answers. I don't need to write the ending of the chapter, mine or theirs. I just need to be silent, and know that the Creator of the universe is in my corner. And that, my friend, is enough for me. You might even call it, security.

7

Comfortable in Your Own Skin

I love my dog. His name is Leo. He is a twenty-pound, caramel-colored bundle of energy. During the course of writing this book, he has been either at my feet or curled up next to me. Every single morning when I come downstairs to greet him, he acts as if he hasn't seen me in months. He can hardly contain his excitement, and that's not just the potty dance talking. This feeling of euphoria isn't exclusive to just me (although I think he loves me the best), Leo acts this way with everyone he meets. Everyone loves Leo. People are glad to see him. He lights up a room and has the ability to make your day better. He even has his own social media account (true story). Leo is a great dog. You know that saying, your greatest strength can also be your greatest weakness? The same is true for my dog. Leo has a problem. He doesn't share the spotlight well with others. He struggles when you don't pay exclusive attention to him. My wife and I can be standing in the kitchen in a warm embrace, and Leo will push his way between us. We call him a "hug hog." We have another smaller dog that we also like to pet from time to time. Leo doesn't handle that well. Inevitably, he will force his way into the other dog's space until you rub his tummy. If you are sitting on the couch, and he needs your attention (which he does), he will take his paw with nails extended and literally grab your arm. Sometimes it's cute, sometimes it's annoying.

I think sometimes we can be like Leo. Have you ever had a conversation with someone who needs the spotlight? That person that has a story to top all stories, to turn any conversation, no matter the topic, back to themselves? I've seen a few impressive "turn of a phrase" moments for someone to get the attention steered back to them. Perhaps you have as well. We all know that insecurity can show up in many different ways. We are going to head down a path in this chapter that could easily feel schizophrenic. How can you be confident and humble without allowing insecurity to take over? I guess that depends on the source of your security.

What is your superpower? Everyone has at least one. I know that sounds like a weird question, especially after the previous paragraph. If I were to ask you to tell me about your good qualities, the areas in your life where you excel, what would they be? I know that may be a difficult question. I also know that if I were to ask you to give me a list of faults, you could easily come up with a list with little effort. Isn't it strange that we find it easier to talk about our downside then the upside of who we are as humans? For a long time, I had this bad habit of downplaying a compliment. When I would sing, people would come up to me and tell me how much they enjoyed it. It was nice to have the compliment, but internally, I would be thinking about how I could have done better here, made the song better there. Sometimes that answer was just in my head; sometimes I said it out loud. It was hard for me to hear people say that I was a good singer even though I am a good at singing. One day, it hit me. It is okay to be good at singing because it is an ability that God gave to me.

> *I praise you, for I am fearfully and wonderfully made. Wonderful are your works; my soul knows it very well. My frame was not hidden from you, when I was being made in secret, intricately woven in the depths of the earth. Your eyes saw my unformed substance; in your book were written, every one of them, the days that were formed for me, when as yet there was none of them.* (Psalm 139:14–16)

God made you the way He made you for a reason. It's easy to read that first verse and say, "Yup, I agree with the *fearfully made* part" and completely miss that you are a gift from God. *You* are a gift from God. You have value. I know that sounds a little bit like Stuart Smalley, but it doesn't make it any less true. Do you see the value that God has created in you? When I downplay it, in a way, I am saying to God that He messed up. Been there, felt that. Let me hit you with some truth. There is only one *you* who will ever walk this earth, even if you are a twin. What does that say about you? What does it say about God? Perhaps we struggle to see the value in us because we don't quite understand the reason for the value.

> *For by the grace given to me I say to everyone among you not to think of himself more highly than he ought to think, but to think with sober judgment, each according to the measure of faith that God has assigned. For as in one body we have many members, and the members do not all have the same function, so we, though many, are one body in Christ, and individually members one of another. Having gifts that differ according to the grace given to us, let us use them: if prophecy, in proportion to our faith; if service, in our serving; the one who teaches, in his teaching; the one who exhorts, in his exhortation; the one who contributes, in generosity; the one who leads, with zeal; the one who does acts of mercy, with cheerfulness.* (Romans 12:3–8)

First, your value comes from God. When you live in that value, it should ultimately point people to Him. Second, your giftedness is a blessing to others. It benefits those around you. Have you ever seen the movie *Chariots of Fire*? There is a scene where Eric Liddell says, "When I run, I feel God's pleasure." He was created by God to run crazy fast. He was also faced with a dilemma in the Olympics. He felt it was wrong to compete on a Sunday, so he chose not to compete on that day. Whether or not you agree with the decision, it highlighted his faith in God and ultimately pointed people to Him. When I sing, I am happy that people enjoy it. But ultimately, I want them to be drawn to God, not me. When I downplay my gift, where does the attention move, to God or to me? Now the reverse is true as well. If I act like I'm all that and a bag of chips, I'm telling God that I got this ability all on my own. Thanks, but I will take it from here God.

Do you see the fine line between humility and pride? Insecurity can push you one way or the other. It is okay to be confident in your superpower as long as it doesn't go against God and it points people back to Him. Let's take another run at this. Where are you gifted? Maybe you are a good listener. You are funny. Perhaps it is your looks or you are really smart. Even though I may not know you personally, I know you have something wonderful about you. I realize you may have grown up in an environment where that was drilled out of you. You've been fed a steady diet of being told you aren't much. I'm sorry that has been in your past, and I am excited to tell you that in your relationship with God, that page can be turned. God adores you. I know that can be difficult to read, but it is so true. God values you so much that He allowed His Son Jesus to die on the cross and pay for your sins so that you can have a personal relationship with Him. If you didn't matter, would God have allowed that to happen? Would Jesus have left heaven and gone through all that torture, humiliation, and, ultimately, death for you if He didn't think you were worth it? Then Jesus rose from the dead. He came back to the very people who abandoned Him because He loved them, because He loves you. Friend, you are valuable. You don't need to hang your head low. You don't need to prove it.

We live in a world where we've decided who is valuable. Most of that is based on money and popularity. The actor in the movie makes way more money than the person who picks up my trash every week, but that doesn't make the movie star more valuable. My garbageman probably doesn't have a ton of followers on social media. I'm guessing that most people on his route don't even know his name. But look at this way, if the famous so-and-so actor didn't come out with a new movie this year, I would be okay. My life would be fine. On the other hand, if the guy who picks up my trash decided to take a year off, it would make my life downright miserable. In my world, the person who picks up my trash is way more valuable to me. That is the beauty of living in the security of God. He has set my value at a pretty high price. Don't let the fleeting call of fame and fortune dictate how you live you your life. Your value doesn't come from the size of your bank account or the number of followers on social media. Instead of wishing you were taller, skinnier, prettier, more outgoing, etc., lean into how you were made because you are the only *you* we got. That's a good thing. Be the best "you" that God has made you to be. It is okay to be secure in who you are and who you are not.

When is the last time you were jealous? Oh come on, it's just us talking here. Was it high school? Was it someone who got a promotion, someone who has a bigger house, perhaps someone who is better dressed? Chances are, if you are a human being, jealously has reared its ugly head in your life. I own a small detailing business where I live. I am a huge car guy. If I had money to burn, I would probably own some very fancy cars. Because of my detailing business, I have clients bring me very exclusive, expensive cars, cars that I would love to own. Sometimes, after watching one of these fancy cars leave my shop, it is hard to get into my normal four-cylinder sedan. The car I drive is a nice, dependable car. It is not a sports car. It does not turn heads when I drive it. It is a regular car. Sometimes I wish I had one of their cars and not mine. You know what I do to make me feel better? I think about the downside of their cars, how expensive they are to insure, their fuel inefficiency, and don't even get me started on the upkeep of maintaining a car like that!

We do that with people too. We think what others have is better. How's this for a truth bomb? Being comfortable in my own skin doesn't mean I have to be uncomfortable with yours. You may want to read that again. We have a tendency to pick apart and tear down other people to feel better about ourselves. If they have less value, that will somehow raise our perceived lack of value. Insecurity allows us do some really dumb things. Let me give you an example. I have been blessed with three amazing women in my life with unique abilities. My wife, Monica, is a gifted interior decorator. Our house looks like a magazine. She has this incredible ability to take the stuff in a room and reposition it so it not only looks good, but also feels comfortable. People enjoy coming to our home. My wife should have her own TV show. My oldest daughter Mackenzie is a gifted cosmetologist. When she was in high school, girls would come to our house and pay her money to fix their hair for prom and other school dances. She has since graduated from college with her business degree and is about to complete her cosmetology degree from a very prestigious school at the top of her class. People in the industry have acknowledged her talent. She is incredible. My younger daughter Madison is a gifted athlete, and by gifted I mean that every sport she tries, not only does she pick it up quickly, but she excels in it. I have watched her go to a state championship in two different sports, one time she won. She also does well in school. She is taking an extra year of college to graduate with two degrees. She is amazing. All of them are gifted, but none of them are threatened by the other talents in our family. The girls ask their mom for help with decorating. We all go to Mackenzie for our hair. We have loved watching Madison in sporting events and are so proud of her college pursuits. Want to know something weird? When my wife is fixing a room, the only input she needs from me is help to move the heavy furniture. No one in my family asks me to color their hair. I'm not consulted by my daughter on her college business classes. Guess what, it's okay. When you are confident in who God made you to be, you are no longer threatened by how God made someone else. Our security comes from God, not from our talent.

I've been known to have a competitive bone or two in my body. I think that can be a good thing. I don't want to give the impression here that we shouldn't try to win, so we just lay down and let others do better. When my girls played sports, I told them, "just do your best." If our best isn't great, work at it. If you aren't growing, you are dying, right? Those are good things that drive us forward. If our security lies in being the best, watch out, because someday there will be someone better. We should strive to do our best. I think that honors God. But be okay with someone else's talent too. Both can coexist. Why is it hard to watch others succeed? Is it because we feel like we are owed what they have? Do we think somehow that God has shorted us and blessed them? We will if that is where we will find our security. Our world is jacked up. We place such a high value on things that cannot last. We strive so hard to get them and then, if we are lucky enough to achieve some of it, we fight tooth and nail to keep it. What if we could be okay with someone else getting ahead? What if we could appreciate who they are, applaud their success, and still lay our head on the pillow at night and be at peace? When my sense of security rises and falls by the success and failures of those around me, I allow them to have way more power in my life than they should.

Years ago, in the early part of my ministry career as a youth pastor, we would take our students to summer camp. This wasn't just any camp, this was one of the largest Christian camps in the country. It was big, like a thousand high school students a week big. There was a waiting list for churches to get into this camp. It was awesome. One of the highlights was finding out who we would have a camp speaker, the person that would speak every night to the students. They usually had big name, well-known speakers. There was a big stage with flashing lights and a cool band that rocked out the room. Every night the students would sit and listen with anticipation to what the camp speaker was going to say. Can I be honest with you? I wanted to be the camp speaker. I'm not proud of this, but there were more than a few times that I would sit in the audience and pull my judgy pants up real high. I would find something that I knew I could do better than the person on stage. I've had people tell me that I am a good communicator. I was, after all, a youth pastor to a very large group of students. Clearly, I should be the camp speaker. Guess what? They never asked me to speak, not once, and I personally knew the guy who picked the camp speakers! I'm embarrassed to say that I wasted energy tearing someone down in my mind while they were on stage, telling high school kids about God. I allowed my own insecurity of thinking I should be on a bigger stage with a bigger audience, doing bigger things to cloud my judgement. I tried to be like God. I thought He was holding out on me. Sounds familiar? The truth is, if God wanted me to be on that stage, do you think He could do it? Do you think the same God who made you and me, hung the stars in space, and told the ocean how far to move forward could also handle putting me on that stage? The answer you are looking for is yes. I think jealousy just reveals areas of our lives where we are trying to find security.

> *Humble yourselves, therefore, under the mighty hand of God so that at the proper time he may exalt you,* (1 Peter 5:6)

Bloom where you are planted. I really like that phrase. It speaks to contentment. What if the reason you didn't have that *thing* was because God was protecting you from you? How about this, what if God is doing something in that person's life and by us getting what they have, we would ruin our story and their story? We either trust God with everything or we trust Him with nothing. We can't pick and choose. That's not trust, it's pride. If I was the camp speaker, I would have robbed that person of living out their giftedness from God. God made them the way He made them for a reason. That's a good thing. It is okay to be happy for someone else. It doesn't lessen you, and it doesn't elevate them. When we choose to live in the security of God, we can be comfortable in our own skin because we are made exactly the way God wanted us to be, which means other people are not a threat to us. They are a blessing. I guess it's all in how you choose to see them and you.

8

The Friends We Keep

Junior High. Two words that strike fear and dread in the heart of every human over the age of fifteen. That magical time in life when you move from the innocence of elementary school where you accept everybody as your friend, to the reality of junior high where your body changes and insecurity rears its ugly head. What is it about that age that causes us to jockey for position and try so hard to fit in and be accepted, no matter the cost? If ever there was a time in your life where insecurity was lived out in relationships, it's here. Many of us take the lessons we learned in our early teens and carry them with us in our adult years. Awesome! We are wired for human relationships, yet we often struggle with making them work. It seems like a cruel joke. The pull of popularity and the need to be needed never really leaves us, even as adults. Insecurity is something that we will deal with until we see Jesus face-to-face. We can't escape it.

So how do we navigate the waters of friendship and our own insecurity? I believe it's a journey, not a destination. But there are some principles we can lean into along the way. People who need people. That's you and me. Relationships are inevitable. I've been blessed with some amazing friendships over in the past five decades of my life. Who are the people who have shaped the person you are today? I think back to when I went off to college as a freshman. I remember showing up in my dorm room and meeting Jim. He was my room-mate all through college. He was also the best man at my wedding. I still laugh about "*taga sacos*." Jim would understand. Even though we live on opposite sides of the country, if he ever needed anything, the answer would be yes. I remember taking my first full-time job as a pastor in Lodi, California. I was a brand-new, very young youth pastor. For thirteen years, our youth staff was our family. They still are today. Significant relationships are woven all through my life. Some of this chapter was written while my wife and I were on a camping trip with friends who still live in California. We both drove halfway to meet together in Oregon. Even though it has been years since I've seen them, we picked back up like it was just last week. I think of my friends here in Washington. The game nights, campfires in the backyard, meals together, the laughter and the tears, and doing living life together, these are the deep, rich relationships we enjoy with great people. I can look back over my life and recount so many wonderful people God brought into my life right when I needed it. Some relationships have stood through time and others were just seasons in my life, but all are meaningful to me. Show me your friends, and I'll show you your future. That is a conversation we've had over and over with our kids. The friends we keep influence how we live our lives. It's a weird dynamic. We were created for a relationship with God, and we were created for relationship with each other. Although I agree we are hardwired with needs of varying levels of connection, in the end, no one goes through life on the solo path. Maybe Barney had it right, "I love you, you love me. We're a happy family!" Sorry, that song is probably stuck in your head now. Sadly, for many of us, this is not the case. We either don't have close friends or the friends we do have aren't really great for us. It's a struggle sometimes to find connection.

What is your purpose for having a friend? Have you ever sat down and thought that out? Do you look at friendship more for what you have to offer or what you want to receive? Although neither of those choices are bad, if they get out of balance, things can go sideways in a hurry. Insecurity shows up often in friendships. I have ruined more than a few relationships because of my insecurity. We've all experienced the desire to be liked, the need to be in control or a compromise to fit in, but if you need to "perform" in order to keep a friend, that's not good for you or for them. Eventually, your bag of tricks will run out and you will be left with a lopsided relationship where you give and give without receiving much in return or you take and take and they run off.

There is a story that Jesus told about a prodigal son. This kid decides he's had enough of dad and the rules in his home, so he demands his inheritance and sets out into the world. He makes friends in the big city and has the time of his life. Since he is loaded, he buys the meals, picks up the bar tab, pays for the hotel, and funds the party. His posse is tight, and they have his back...until the money runs out. When he stops giving to the relationship, they stop being his friend. The prodigal son goes from the penthouse to the pigpen, literally, and finds a job feeding pigs just so he can survive. He ran out of money, and coincidentally, his friends ran out on him. Have you ever had an experience like that? Maybe you are the person on the other side of that story. Your friendships are all about what you get out of them. You are on the receiving end of the emotional support or maybe even the financial support of others. The scales are mostly tipped in your favor. When your relationships are no longer benefiting you, it's time to move on. Perhaps it's your friends who keep moving on, and you don't seem to understand why. So what do we do? I think the best thing is for you and I to start with "numero uno" and take an unfiltered look in the mirror. If we were choosing someone to be a friend, would we make our own list?

What do you look for in a friend? What are your top three qualities? Mine are loyalty, honesty, and empathy. Close friends aren't always easy to find. It takes work. Have you ever heard the saying "Like attracts like"? It's the idea that who you are and the values you hold will be the very things that attract other people to you. Whether you are outgoing or introverted, honest or gossipy, rude or kind, you probably have those type of people close by. The Bible says it this way, "Do not be deceived: 'Bad company ruins good morals'" (1 Corinthians 15:33). Which side of this verse best reflects you? What type of relationships do you attract or perhaps repel? I know that's a hard question to answer. If I want friends who are loyal, then I need to be loyal. If I want friends who are honest, then I need to be honest. Proverbs 13:20 says, "Whoever walks with the wise becomes wise, but the companion of fools will suffer harm." Proverbs 27:17 says, "Iron sharpens iron, and one man sharpens another." No matter how hard I try, I cannot sharpen an axe with a stick of butter. It just won't work. Living out of insecurity does not attract secure people. The good ones may stick around for a while, some may even love you enough to have a "tough talk" with you, but if you head down that path long enough, you will eventually push them away. Insecurity attracts insecurity. I have talked to more people who wonder why they keep messing up in life. They make the same bad decisions over and over again. Look around. Are the friends in your life sharpening you? Remember that the people around you have influence in your life just like you have influence on their life. My dad used to say if you want to fly like an eagle, don't run around with turkeys. That door swings both ways. Sometimes I'm the eagle; sometimes I'm the turkey.

I believe that in every relationship there are two significant *E*s that are constantly in play, expectations, and emotional currency. Allow me to explain. Right now, you are deep into this book. When you picked it up, you had certain expectations about what you would find inside the cover. The fact that you are reading these words means that so far, this book is meeting the expectations you had when you picked it up. Think of a relationship that you enjoy. Perhaps it's your marriage, a close friend, or maybe a coworker or neighbor across the street. Believe it or not, you have a set of expectations in that relationship with them that they are currently providing in your life. It works because your expectations are being met. I don't mean that you are being selfish or self-absorbed. It's just a fact. Think about a time you had a disagreement with that person. What was the root cause? Was it that you had a certain expectation that the other person failed to meet? This is a normal dance that we do in our relationships. We grow closer or further apart based on our expectations. Think of a relationship that ended. What expectation did you have that wasn't met? Was it trust that was broken? Was it lack of intimacy? Did they stop being available? Whatever it was, when those expectations are not being met, we voice them—sometimes with words, sometimes with actions.

Have you ever heard that your greatest strength is also your greatest weakness? For me, loyalty is huge. I am fiercely loyal in my relationships. You mess with my friends, you mess with me. That can be great when you are "in" with me. But the downside is that if I feel your loyalty toward me has been violated, you can quickly be "out." Loyalty can easily become a piece of *security* in my life, a piece of me that I try to control. This is where I need to lean into the pivot of security versus insecurity. Humans hurt each other, whether intentionally or not. I need to take a realistic look at my expectations of other people. First, am I asking this person to fulfill a need that is unfair or self-serving to my own needs? It isn't difficult at all to put a human relationship in place of my relationship with God. Am I asking them to provide something for me that only God can provide? Our security can only reside in our relationship with God, not people. People will let you down because they are sinful. I let people down for the same reason. When we try to place our security in human relationships, we are placing unrealistic expectations on them. A human relationship can never bring the same security we get from God. It's not possible. Is it okay to have secure relationships with people? I think so. I love my wife, I love my daughters, and I know they love me. There is security in those words. Here is the flip side of that statement. I have disappointed them, and they have disappointed me. We have let each other down. We all have certain expectations in our relationship. Most of the time they are met, but sometimes they are not. This is where our relationship with God is so critical.

I look to God to be a better husband and father. I look to the Bible for wisdom and guidance. Some of the expectations I have for my wife and daughters are selfish. Some of their expectations of me fall into the same category. That's why we look to God. When our security comes from our relationship with God, we will view our relationships differently. We can't help it. Here is what I know to be true in my life. I have expectations in every relationship. When conflict comes in those relationships, it is because an expectation I have with them hasn't been met. I have to check myself to see if my expectations are based on "me" or "we." What is my motivation? For example, a mutually beneficial expectation in a relationship is trust. That's a realistic expectation that benefits both. An unrealistic expectation that my friend's entire life revolves around me and is always available to meet my needs is only beneficial to me. Some of you may be thinking, "Wait, that's a bad thing?" My motivation is to place my security in a person so I feel better about myself. If your security comes from anything else other than your relationship with God, it will fail. So how do we make it work with other people? That brings me to the second *E*, emotional currency.

Have you ever bounced a check? It's a tough lesson to learn. Just because you have checks in the checkbook doesn't mean you have money in your account to cover them. Bouncing a check can be expensive. Depending on your bank, you could pay a bunch of fees in addition to messing up your credit. You bounce a check because you haven't made enough deposits in your account to cover the check you are about to write. It only works if you put in enough to cover what you take out. Relationships work on the same principle. We are constantly making deposits and withdrawals with people. I think that shows up most prevalently in a marriage. When I give my wife compliments, make the bed (sometimes), buy her flowers, or put the dishes in the dishwasher, I am making emotional deposits in her life. That's a good thing. There are times, however, when I make a withdrawal from her emotional account. Can I be honest with you? I have a problem closing cupboards. I don't know why. Maybe I was absent from school the day they taught us that lesson. My wife asks me to close them,

71

and I want to, but often I forget. We even had those soft close hinges installed, so if I just push them, they will automatically close (true story). My cabinet problem can be a source of frustration to my wife. When she walks in the kitchen and sees them open, I withdraw from my wife's emotional bank. Depending on the day or the amount of frequency, some of those checks I write can be quite large.

Every relationship is a series of emotional deposits and withdrawals. It's the normal dance we do with one another. Give and take. If I am living in insecurity, I am probably writing way more checks. If I am looking to a person to give me my security, it will be exhausting to the person on the other side of me. Have you ever seen teenagers in love? That whole "Do you like me? Check the box yes or no" thing. Their immaturity can cause them to very easily obsess over every interaction, analyze every word in a note or text, and see other friendships as a threat to their happiness. They need to be with them constantly. The need to be needed and needing constant reassurance that their needs are being met comes off as, well, needy. Have you ever seen that played out with adults? It isn't pretty. When I am living securely in God. I see relationships as a compliment to my life, not the center of it. Coincidently, I don't want someone else to see me as the center of their universe, no matter how good it feels. Do I want my wife to love me? You bet I do! That is a relationship I need to nurture every single day. Do I want my wife to see me as her sole source of security? Nope. Why? Because I sometimes I leave the cupboards open. I let her down. I'm a sinner, and I'm selfish. God has to be first in her life, period. Otherwise, she can't be the wife I need. The same is true for me. Human relationships are meant to complement our relationship with God, not replace it. If I can put this in human terms, I can't bounce a check with God. His resources are limitless. In my human relationships, I will continue to make emotional deposits and withdrawals. Some days are better than others. If I am constantly writing emotional checks with the people in my life, eventually those relationships will be bankrupt. Healthy relationships make more deposits and less withdrawals so they can weather the storm when a big check needs to be cashed.

You probably heard the saying, "Be the person you want others to be for you." It really is that simple. Take a minute to think about that statement. What does a healthy friendship, relationship, or marriage look like? The best place to start is asking God to set you on the right path. He is the Creator of relationships. That makes Him the ultimate authority on the subject. He gave us guidelines in the Bible. That is the litmus test to check your motives and actions in every relationship. If you need a reference, read 1 Corinthians 13. I used to think the Bible was a bunch of rules and regulations. I've learned since then that the Bible is God's love letter to us on how to navigate this life with Him and with other people. Some of what you want from others isn't good for you or them. A second step is to find some people around you who are a little further down the road than you and ask them for advice. I want to be clear that if someone's advice doesn't line up with the Bible, move on. If you have been in relationships long enough, you will eventually encounter conflict. It is inevitable. The goal is restoration. Some of my greatest growth moments have been when a friend has looked me in the eye and told me some tough truths. That is the blessing of someone who wants the best for you, not for them.

I've also had moments when people have told me things that were not truth, that were not done in love, and that was all about them feeling better about themselves. Sometimes they don't even talk to you directly. They talk around you. It hurts. It wounds the soul. Often the knee-jerk reaction is to defend yourself, to retaliate against them, to defend your honor. Those are the moments you have to lean deep into your security with God. Remember, we live in a broken world with broken people who do broken things. There will be times when you realize you need to walk away from a friendship for a season, maybe longer. When that happens, check with God, check yourself and then take the high road. Talk to your friend. Be kind. Remember, God is writing all of our stories. You are not responsible for their actions. You are only responsible for how you respond to their actions. Who knows what God will do through you in their life, if you do it correctly. Relationships are a risk worth taking. We all survived junior high. Yes, there are ups and downs, but that's part of the blessing. When we lean into our security in God, we will see them differently. Take the journey. Choose to be the iron that sharpens iron, not the stick of butter.

9

Being a Victim, Less

I want to start this chapter by acknowledging that for some of you, you should skip down a couple of paragraphs. Some of you have experienced some truly traumatic events in your life. Being the victim of something is serious. It can take years to move past it. I understand. That is not what this chapter is all about. There may be some that will read this and immediately point to a person and situation and say, "I can't believe you wrote this!" I would say that you are correct. There are always exceptions to everything. I've been the victim of trauma, and I am no expert on how someone should move forward. There are way better books you can read for that. I would also say that if your first reaction to reading "being a victim, less" is criticism, excuses, and loopholes, you are definitely the person that should read everything in this chapter, maybe twice. Okay, deep breath. Here we go.

Since we have been together this far, I think I can safely say that we are friends, or at least strong acquaintances. This chapter might get a little rough. Scratch that, this chapter will get a little rough. If you and I really want to live securely in our relationship with God, we need to do a little soul searching. I wrote the title to this chapter years ago. I think it is more applicable today than it was then. I think this chapter is probably the biggest hurdle for people, especially in working through their insecurity. So let's jump in the deep end together because there is something we all need to hear. Ready? The world is not out to get you. People do not go out of their way every day thinking up ways to make your life miserable. Stop being offended so much. It's time to be a victim, less.

Let me tell you about my journey. Years ago, I walked into my therapist's office and began our session with this statement, "Jeff, I don't want to be a victim anymore. I've spent too much time focusing on what has been done to me. Help me stop being a victim." My therapist responded back to me with something that would change my life. He looked at me and said, "Kevin, do you believe that God can be your advocate, that God will stand up for you, that He is for you?" I believed it in my head, but in my heart...well, that was a struggle. The truth is, I feel the need to tell my side of the story. My voice must be heard! My rights supersede your logic. Focusing on my perceived rights means I don't have to consider my responsibility in the situation. It is about what you did to me and how we resolve it so I feel better. Can I let you in on a little secret? Feelings lie. Living securely in my relationship with God means I trust Him with everything, even when I'm offended. Earlier, we talked about forgiveness and what this looks like when it comes to me and other people. In this chapter, I want us to take a look at our side of the ledger. You know how sometimes people can be jerks? The truth is, so can we. The society we live in today has become an intolerant, victim-first mentality. When is the last time you heard a sincere, "I own it" apology? It might take you a minute.

I'm the youngest of four. Growing up, I wasn't super close to my siblings. There's a bit of an age gap. They grew up together, while I lagged behind a few years. By the time I hit high school, I was the only child in the home. Let me be clear about something. I had a pretty good childhood. My parents stayed married. They were good providers. I had a family. I went to church almost every week. I was popular. I was a decent athlete. I had a really good singing voice. I was even the vice president of my senior class. Not bad. I also had some bad things happen. Both of my grandfathers died within six months of each other. I lived in the shadow of my older and very accomplished siblings who went to the same small "everyone knows you" school before me. I was picked on. I was lonely. I had my heart broken. I tried really hard to keep friends. I was sexually molested. Yup, I don't want that last statement to overshadow everything else. It is a part of my story, but it isn't the entire book. Why am I telling you all of this? We all experience bad and good in our formative years. Some more of one or less of the other, but no one comes through unscathed. We take those experiences into our adult years. Some of those things are good, some are bad. What I've realized is that many of the experiences we've had as a kids are duplicated in our adult years. The names and faces may change, but the carousel still goes round and round. I wanted to get off the carousel. The question is, do you?

Have you ever been stuck somewhere? One time in junior high, I was flying home from camp with a friend of mine. Our flight got cancelled. My dad was a commercial pilot so as a kid I had been in lots of airports, but I was always with an adult. At first, my friend and I thought it was pretty cool. Two kids in an airport, waiting for the next flight, what could go wrong? Then we found out we had to spend the night in the airport, by ourselves, in New Jersey. Remember, this was before cell phones, iPads, and the TSA. Can I just say that there are a lot of interesting people that roam around the airport in the middle of the night. Our confidence quickly turned to nervousness, which snowballed into straight up fear. Eventually, we just were exhausted. When morning came and we boarded our flight, we just collapsed on the airplane. The fun had worn off. We just wanted the security of our own bed. Have you ever been *stuck* emotionally? I have. It feels a lot like my night in the airport. At first, you feel confident, "I got this." Then it turns to nervous energy which looks a lot like fear. Eventually, you are just exhausted. When something bad happens to you, who do you tell? How many people do you involve in your story? I'm not talking about going to a trusted friend for advice or empathy. I mean how often do people hear the story of when so-and-so did such-and-such to you? Insecurity can easily try to make you the hero of your story. Honestly, some "stories" need to be chapters that are read, then turn the page and just move on in the book.

I want to be careful here because this is not a one-size-fits-all discussion. I do want to try and keep it on a broad level, but in saying that I also want to acknowledge that being a victim of something is not just a "rub some dirt on it and move on" solution. Being a victimized by someone else is a traumatic experience. I was the victim of sexual assault as a child. It was something that happened to me. It was bad, it should not have happened, and it left me with some scars. I needed to deal with what happened to me. Those are all real things. Here is what I mean about having a victim mentality. If I use what happened to me as a kid as an excuse for bad behavior as an adult, if every time I offend or act out and I blame it on being molested, I am living as a victim. I'm stuck because I use a terrible event as an excuse for my unwillingness to change. What happened to me as a child was a chapter in my life, it isn't my whole story. Being a victim of something allows me to divert the attention off of my behavior and attempt to move the responsibility on to someone or something else.

If you grew up in a home where everyone yelled all the time, there is a chance you may have leanings toward acting out in anger. It was modeled in your childhood and is now being played out as an adult. Just because you grew up in that environment doesn't give you a pass to act out in anger if things don't go your way. At some point, you have to take responsibility "for you" and stop focusing on what happened "to you." I grow weary of forty-year-old adults who still blame all their problems on their parents. Stop it. You've been an adult longer than you were a kid under their roof. Your parents aren't making you *do* anything. You are making you do things. Insecurity puts the focus on what has happened to you as a form of control. Maybe you want attention. Maybe you want empathy. There are more productive ways to get it. If I can't control my circumstances, then I must be a victim of them, which is just another way of trying to gain control. It doesn't work. The house of cards eventually comes tumbling down. Trust me.

Okay, that was tough. I may have offended some of you. If not, this next part just might do it. Let me ask you something, when was the last time you owned your mistakes? I'm talking about the *please forgive me I'm owning my part of the ledger* kind of conversation. Do you know the difference between saying I'm sorry and asking for forgiveness? Saying sorry is easy. It's not that big of a deal. If I bump into you in the store, I'd say, "Oh, I'm sorry." It's an unintentional offense. Asking for forgiveness is bigger than that. It's a release of control. I am owning my mistake and giving you the power by asking you to forgive me. The scary part is that they may choose to say no. This too can be a dicey situation because sometimes people who are in abusive relationships can own something that isn't their fault because they are so wrapped up in the perceived security of the abusive relationship, they will keep running back for more. If that is you, if you are in any type of abusive relationship, you need to get away from it right now. Tell a trusted friend. Call a hotline number. Go to your local church. Don't live in the darkness. There is help for you. The person I want to talk to is the one who can always find a way to make their mistakes seem like someone else's fault. The one who needs to be right all the time. Those who are quickly offended that someone may not see the world the same way as they do. If you don't know what I'm talking about, head to any online news article and scroll down the comments. No matter what the story, someone is offended. More than that, they are offended that you are offended at them being offended. We are so quick to point out the wrongs of others, to tear them down to build us up. We seek the approval of strangers to feel better and can absolutely lose our minds at the person who dares to disagree. Why is that? What is the harm in letting things go? We've lost the ability of being able to disagree without being disagreeable. The Bible talks about removing the plank out of our own eye instead of being hyper-focused on the speck in someone else's eye. Have you ever considered that you may be part of your own problem? It's easy to be the victim and blame someone else. It's hard to take responsibility for our actions. I know, I know, but they are wrong! Someone has to tell them!

When my security rests in God, I don't need to win. God has that handled. You may be the first person to show them kindness instead of hate. If you are wrong, say it. If you messed up, own it. You won't find security in pointing out the perceived faults you find in others. Sometimes you need to have difficult conversations, kind of like the one we are having now. When it is done in love, the *win* will be found in being *for* the other person's good, not being right. Why do bad things happen to good people? Man, if I had a dollar for every time I've been asked that question as a pastor. I've said this before, but it bears repeating. We live in a broken world with broken people who do broken things. There are times when you are on the receiving end of someone else's bad behavior.

I remember one time when my wife called me on the phone, telling me she was just in an accident on the freeway. She was driving in our minivan with our two little girls when she was broadsided and knocked off the road by another vehicle. Driving up to that scene was terrifying. Watching my wife being loaded into an ambulance was awful. We found out later at the hospital that the other driver was drunk. We were fortunate that everyone in my family made it home that evening. Our minivan was totaled, but everyone was alive. To this day, that accident still has an impact on my wife when she is in the car. My family was driving down the road and was the victim of someone else's bad behavior. Why? I don't know. I think we have this idea in our heads that bad things should happen to bad people and good things should happen to good people. When they don't, somehow God was asleep at the wheel. I guess my first response to that is, what is your definition of good? I love my wife and girls, but they are not perfect. None of us are. How about this. Jesus was good. Complete perfection. He walked this earth and never sinned. Jesus explained it this way:

> *I have said these things to you, that in me you may have peace. In the world you will have tribu-lation. But take heart; I have overcome the world.*
> (John 16:33)

Do you know what people did to Jesus? They killed Him. God allowed that to happen for our good. Jesus needed to die to pay the price of our sins and rise from the dead to defeat sin and death. This was needed so we could have a relationship with God (see chapter 2). In this world, we will have trouble, it's a guarantee.

Calling versus circumstances—it is all a matter of perspective and where you choose to place your focus. It really comes down to what do you believe about God. There is a verse tattooed on my arm that is a constant reminder that God is *for me*. It is hard to believe that when bad things happen *to me*. Somehow I have equated my circumstances in life to how God views me. Nothing could be further from the truth. I believe that God has a plan for my life. It is a "God good" plan, which is very different than a "Kevin good" plan. God sees the entire span of my life. Psalm 139 tells me that God was writing the pages of my story before I was even born. God has called me into a relationship with Him. That is my security. When bad things happen to me, especially when it is caused by someone else's brokenness, it is very tempting to focus on my circumstances. Why did this happen to me? I don't deserve this. People get cancer, cars get hit by drunk drivers, a little boy was molested, bad things will happen in this life. Remember, it's a broken world with broken people who do broken things. I believe it is what you do and how you react when those things happen that makes all the difference.

There is a little phrase in the book of Job that I passed by for years. I didn't understand the significance until it was pointed out to me. Job 42:16 says, "And after this...." Most of us know the story of Job. Terrible things happened to him then eventually everything was restored. Most people never get to that part of their story, the "and after this." We get so focused on what is happening to us that we lose sight of the One who has it all under control. I recently had a conversation with my mom about this very point. When I do bad things, I want God's mercy on me, but when someone else does bad things, especially bad things to me, I want God's wrath on them.

I quickly lose sight that God is writing everyone's story, not just mine. That is a hard pill to swallow, especially when something bad happens to me through no fault of my own. The hope is that people will make things right, but even if they don't, I'm only responsible for my reaction to their action. When I choose to live securely in my relationship with God, it makes bad things easier to navigate not because they hurt less, but rather because God is with me when I go through them. That's what it means when God is for me. He has a plan for my life, and it is a good plan. His version of good is higher and wiser than mine. His version of good may weave my story with someone else. His version of good takes into account my mistakes and the mistakes of others. All God is asking me to do is lean into Him.

During the process of writing this book, I've had a song on con-stant loop. It helped me concentrate. The song is called "Even If" by Mercy Me. Here's the chorus:

> *I know You're able, and I know You can*
> *Save through the fire with Your mighty hand*
> *But even if You don't*
> *My hope is You alone*
> *I know the sorrow, and I know the hurt*
> *Would all go away if You'd just say the word*
> *But even if You don't*
> *My hope is You alone*

It isn't about getting through life with the least amount of pain possible. Some of the darkest days of my life has been my greatest moments of growth. God is for you. God is for me. That is truth, and I trust it.

I've been thinking a lot about this chapter and the hang-ups this one topic cause in so many of us. This morning, I was sitting on the back porch with my wife and my dog, and I came across this verse in my Bible. I don't think it was by accident that today of all days, as I finish up this chapter, God placed it before me.

> *But he said to me, "My grace is sufficient for you, for my power is made perfect in weakness." Therefore I will boast all the more gladly of my weaknesses, so that the power of Christ may rest upon me. For the sake of Christ, then, I am content with weaknesses, insults, hardships, persecutions, and calamities. For when I am weak, then I am strong.* (2 Corinthians 12:9–10)

When bad things happen—and they will; whether they are caused by me, by others, or a combination of both; I know that God is for me, and that He has it all under control. I think that is how we become victims, less.

10

Big Kingdom versus little kingdom

This is one of those moments I thought might never happen, the writing of the last chapter. It doesn't feel like I'm crossing the finish line, more like passing the mile marker on a very long lap. The good thing is that I have better information to navigate the course the next time around. I hope you do too.

Insecurity is not something you overcome, it is something you manage. Life is full of good and bad days. The trick is how you navigate the in-betweens. When we live in the security of our relationship with God, the bad days, the moments we cannot control, can produce peace in the midst of the storm. Listen to the promise in Psalm 91:1–2, "He who dwells in the shelter of the Most High will abide in the shadow of the Almighty. I will say to the LORD, 'My refuge and my fortress, my God, in whom I trust.'" This isn't a *one and done* type of reminder. It's a place you live in every single day. Living in God's security changes our perspective. It has to. The by-product of insecurity is having a very self-centered view of the world. We process things based on our feelings and how everything affects us. When I believe the source of my security comes from me and what I do, self-centeredness is sure to follow. Protect my little kingdom.

Let me ask you something, what's your kingdom? We all have them. I'm curious as to what yours might be. Ask yourself this question. What sets you off the quickest? What is your pressure point? What are you quick to defend? We all have little kingdoms, the place where we go to be in control. Read that verse again. You and I cannot dwell in God's shelter and at the same time try to defend our kingdom. It doesn't work. If you want to live more securely, let go of your little kingdom. It won't give you what you want. You already know that. Look, I know it isn't as easy as saying, "Okay, God, here you go." I still go back and check on things in my little kingdom. I'm getting better at going there less and not staying as long, but the temptation is still there. God can either handle everything or He can handle nothing. He isn't a part-time God. When we learn to live more in His Security, we begin to understand the bigger picture. The Big Kingdom. God's Kingdom.

> *So we do not lose heart. Though our outer self is wasting away, our inner self is being renewed day by day. For this light momentary affliction is preparing for us an eternal weight of glory beyond all comparison, as we look not to the things that are seen but to the things that are unseen. For the things that are seen are transient, but the things that are unseen are eternal.* (2 Corinthians 4:16–18)

"It's not about you." I love that first line in the book *The Purpose Driven Life* by Rick Warren. Truer words have never been said. We live in a world that tells us it is all about us. We are the center of our universe. That is the problem. We focus all of our attention on our little kingdoms. Protect that, and security will follow.

Have you ever met someone who can't stop talking about themselves? Yes, I'm talking about *that* person. It's hard to be around that person for any length of time. Eventually, the stories start looping around, especially when a new person comes into the group. Now think about someone who is humble. Chances are, this task will be more difficult to complete. People who are humble care more about others than themselves. They don't need to share their resume with the world. They are easy to be around because they put people at ease. Insecure people put others on edge. It's hard to have a relationship with an insecure person. Read Philippians 2:3–4, "Do nothing from selfish ambition or conceit, but in humility count others more significant than yourselves. Let each of you look not only to his own interests, but also to the interests of others." On our own, you and I are not capable of pulling this off. This is Big Kingdom stuff. We know how to do the *passive-aggressive do something nice for someone to manipulate them so they like me or will come my way* but that's not what this verse is saying. Selfish ambition, conceit, control— that's our little kingdom talking right there. Humility, holding others in high regard, looking out for their best interests with no strings attached—that's Big Kingdom stuff. The passage goes on, "Have this mind among yourselves, which is yours in Christ Jesus, who, though he was in the form of God, did not count equality with God a thing to be grasped, but emptied himself, by taking the form of a servant, being born in the likeness of men. And being found in human form, he humbled himself by becoming obedient to the point of death, even death on a cross" (Philippians 2:5–8).

Jesus emptied Himself for us. Fully God, He set that aside to serve mankind to the point of dying on the cross for our sins and rising from the dead so that we could have a personal relationship with God. He did all of that so you and I could live securely in that relationship. See how this comes full circle? Jesus emptied Himself, meaning that although He had every right, He chose to set that aside to serve us. The Bible tells us to have the same mindset. When I am living securely in my relationship with God, I don't need to say or do things to provide my own security. I already have it in Christ. I don't need to *win* an argument. I can *love* my enemies. It isn't about me. The goal isn't to find our security here on earth, but rather to share the security we have found in Christ. I have wasted so much time and energy establishing my little kingdoms thinking that the next one will be the best one. They never are. Never.

I turned fifty this year. I remember when my mom turned the big 5-0. I asked her what it was like to be half a century old and know that three quarters of your life is now behind you. I know, I know, cut me some slack, I'm the baby in my family. At the time, I thought I was hilarious. Now that I'm here, it's not quite as funny. I told my wife that I feel like I'm old enough now that people will listen to me but still young enough to be relevant. Why does that matter? Because if I could change one thing in my life, one thing that would have saved me and those around me a bunch of heartache, it would be this—live securely in a personal relationship with God. Everything else flows from that. We spend so much time pursuing little kingdom stuff, things that don't really matter in view of our moment in history on this earth. Should you have goals, aspirations, pursue dreams? Absolutely! There is nothing wrong with that as long as you have the correct filter. Whose *kingdom* are you trying to secure?

I came across a verse that I have read a bunch of times in my life. It didn't really have that much of an impact on me before. Maybe it's my age or maybe it's this book, but this verse really stopped me in my tracks. The apostle Paul, a man who early in his life was very much pursuing his own little kingdoms and who also met Jesus in a very up close and personal way (see Acts 9), was writing a letter to the church in Philippi. Here's what he said, "What you have learned and received and heard and seen in me—practice these things, and the God of peace will be with you" (Philippians 4:9). I read that and thought, *Could I write something like that?* Paul wasn't saying that he had arrived as a human. He hadn't achieved perfection here on earth. That's impossible. He was still a sinner, just like you and me. What I find interesting about that verse was that Paul was saying that he wanted his life to point people back to Jesus. He was saying that it wasn't about him, it was about Christ in his life. It was about God's Kingdom, not his kingdom.

I want to ask you a question, where do you have influence? Everyone has influence. Need proof? What would happen if you walked into a crowded restaurant and started running around yelling that the building was on fire? People would absolutely react to your influence on their lives. So let me ask you again, where do you have influence? Are you married? Do you have kids? Do you work somewhere or have a social media account? All of the people who are on the other side of you as you live your life are people that you influence. Sit in that thought for just a minute. Now I want you to read that verse again, "What you have learned and received and heard and seen in me—practice these things, and the God of peace will be with you" (Philippians 4:9).

Two things I know to be true about you: you are a person of influence and God has placed you in the lives of those people around you for a reason. That's Big Kingdom stuff right there! How you and I choose to live our lives in the up and down moments is seen by those around us. I can hear you muttering back to me, "Great, Kevin! Thanks a lot! Life is hard enough without that pressure!" Remember what Rick Warren said, "It's not about you." Life is hard sometimes, and life is good sometimes. How we act and react in those moments is important. Have you ever seen someone who has a relationship with Christ go through something difficult? People wonder how they can stay so calm. Have you seen someone go through something good and their reaction is to thank God for His provision? The goal is to live securely in our relationship with God on the upside or the downside. Is perfection the goal? Nope, that's impossible. I believe the goal is to live in such a way that we point people to the same place where we get our security. Fail forward. We are just beggars telling other beggars where we found bread. Point them to Jesus. How is that possible? Let's look at what else Paul said.

I remember the day that my father-in-law told us of his diagnosis of cancer. It was Memorial Day weekend, and we had gathered at their house for a family event. I don't really remember how he told us, but I do remember the prayer he prayed. As we all stood in a circle, He asked God for healing, of course, but with equal urgency, he asked God to help him point people back to Jesus, no matter what the outcome. He died ten weeks later, and God honored his request.

My father-in-law lived out his days telling people that he was leaving this earth soon. He knew where he would spend eternity and he wanted others to know Jesus just like he did. All these years later, I still remember it like it just happened. If you are wondering how that is possible, let me point you back to Paul's previous comments to the church in Philippi:

> *Rejoice in the Lord always; again I will say, rejoice. Let your reasonableness be known to everyone. The Lord is at hand; do not be anxious about anything, but in everything by prayer and supplication with thanksgiving let your requests be made known to God. And the peace of God, which surpasses all understanding, will guard your hearts and your minds in Christ Jesus.* (Philippians 4:4–7)

Before Paul wrote, "What you have learned and received and heard and seen in me," he explained how to do it. When our security comes from God, we will live our lives in a different way. When my father-in-law got his diagnosis, he wasn't "rejoicing" in his circumstances, but he was glad that God was in control of all of it. There is joy in that Hope. Paul goes on to say that we shouldn't be anxious about anything. WHAT! How is that even possible? What is anxiety at its root? A reaction to something I cannot control. Sounds a lot like insecurity. What's the cure for anxiety? Giving the things that causing you anxiety, things you want to control but know you cannot, over to God. What happens when we do that? "And the peace of God, which surpasses all understanding, will guard your hearts and your minds in Christ Jesus" (Philippians 4:7). Peace. God's peace. Security. It's not the absence of trouble, but rather the security of knowing that God is with you in the midst of it. I've experienced that in my own life and I have seen it played out in the lives of others. Not only will God give you peace, but He will also guard your heart and your mind *in Christ Jesus.* Why is that so important? Let me go back to my father-in-law.

After he retired from his career, he didn't want to sit around the house so he worked as a courtesy driver for a car dealership. He was loved there. People could see a difference in his life. When he told his co-workers he had cancer, he also let them know of the peace he had because of his relationship with God. Those people got to see his faith in God lived out before their very eyes. Do you think that had an impact on them? He used his influence with others to point them to God. He did this when things were going well, and he did it when things were not going well. After he died, the dealership created an employee of the year award in his honor that is still given out to this day. That's influence. So how do we do it? How do we actually live it out? Paul goes on to say this:

> *Finally, brothers, whatever is true, whatever is honorable, whatever is just, whatever is pure, whatever is lovely, whatever is commendable, if there is any excellence, if there is anything worthy of praise, think about these things.* (Philippians 4:8)

How's your mind? When you start to feel insecure, what are the thoughts that start running through your head? Do any of these words make the list? What would happen if you and I started applying these things to our thought process when those feelings of insecurity come into play? Would it make a difference? Absolutely. Remember the pattern. I feel insecure so I make decisions to control my environment to feel more secure, but since those things won't ultimately provide me with security and they fail me (which they will), I am left feeling worse than when I started. That's how my kingdom works, patterns of false security that breed more insecurity. When I rest in the security of my relationship with God, there will be peace, no matter what I face in life. People notice that. We all know what insecurity looks like. We've seen it in our lives and the lives of others. That's normal. Watching someone who is resting in God, that is definitely different. That's pointing people to God's kingdom.

SECURE ME

I love music. It has helped many, many times in my life. A few years ago, I came across a song that truly capture the story of my life. It's called "Scars" by I Am They.

Waking up to a new sunrise
Looking back from the other side
I can see now with open eyes,

Darkest water and deepest pain
I wouldn't trade it for anything,
'Cause my brokenness brought me to You
And these wounds are a story You'll use

So I'm thankful for the scars
'Cause without them I wouldn't know Your heart
And I know they'll always tell of who You are
So forever I am thankful for the scars

Now I'm standing in confidence
With the strength of Your faithfulness
And I'm not who I was before
No, I don't have to fear anymore

So I'm thankful for the scars
'Cause without them I wouldn't know Your heart
And I know they'll always tell of who You are,
So forever I am thankful for the scars

I can see, I can see
How You delivered me
In Your hands, in Your feet,
I found my victory

I'm thankful for Your scars
'Cause without them I wouldn't know Your heart
And with my life, I'll tell of who You are
So forever I am thankful for the scars

I wept when I heard this song. I don't know where you are today or what you are facing. If you have read this far, there is a good chance you've been struggling with something. Oh, friend, if I could put my arm around you today in your moment of insecurity, I would play this song and tell you about the difference Jesus has made in my life. I haven't always seen what God was doing while it was happening, but as I look back, I can so see the hand of God moving in my life, protecting me and pursuing me, even when I was looking everywhere else for my security. I hope today you understand how much God loves you. I hope today you are a follower of Jesus. I hope today you are living in a relationship with Him. It is the single most important decision you will ever make in your life. It is who you were always meant to be. It is the security you were always meant to have. No matter how hard you try to find security on your own, I promise you, you will always come back to this very spot. I have never once regretted having a relationship with God. And the regrets that I have had about foolish pursuits to gain something that was impossible, God has helped with those as well. Is it possible to live securely? Yes, it is, but only in the security God can give. When we do that, it not only changes our life, it will change the lives of those around us as well. Families will be different, marriages will be different, social media will be different because we will be different. That's how the security that God offers to all changes our world and the world around us. Security isn't a destination, it's a journey, and one that is worth pursuing. I hope over the pages of this book, some of my story has helped you with yours. I think that is how it is supposed to work. I wish I knew then what I know now. I believe that's how God can turn our mistakes into blessings. I hope you will continue to pursue God's security and leave your insecurity behind. It's a load we were never meant to carry. Live securely in Him. Every. Single. Day. You won't regret it.

You know "that conversation" every parent has with their kid right before they head off to summer camp or the first day of school or college? That speech they give where they try to remember to say all the things they need to say right before you leave. This feels a little like that moment. There are so many things I feel like I want to say before this book is complete. But since I've been on the receiving and giving end of those speeches, I'll keep it simple. One of my absolute favorite verses in the Bible is John 10:10, "I came that they may have life, and have it abundantly." It's Jesus speaking directly to you and to me. He came to this earth to bring "life," salvation, and restoration of a relationship with God through Him. Then He goes on to say, "And have it abundantly." In the original Greek, it means "to be overwhelmed, an abundance, more than you could possibly need." Jesus isn't talking about more salvation, that is a onetime event. He is talking about our personal relationship with God—a deep, rich, and overflowing more-than-you-could-possibly-imagine relationship with God right now. Think of it in the context of security. Think of what it can be like today, right now, to live in deep rich overflowing more than you could possibly imagine security in God. You can. Today. When people see that in you, they see God working in you, and that's what it's all about. Go live it for you and for them and see how God works through all of it. That is what I wish for you as you close this book. Live your SECURE ME life abundantly.

It is who you and I were always meant to be.

About the Author

Kevin Scruggs is a pastor in the Pacific Northwest where he lives with his best friend and wife, Monica, their two dogs, and the cat. They have two adult daughters who love their dad very much and would describe him as a man who isn't afraid to laugh at his own jokes, even if he laughs alone.

Kevin has been in ministry for over thirty years and has a master's degree in biblical counseling. He is on a lifelong journey of connecting with people and pointing them to the One who has made all the difference in his life, Jesus.

CPSIA information can be obtained
at www.ICGtesting.com
Printed in the USA
FSHW022257090222
88209FS